Fodor's POCKET first edition

martha's vineyard

fodor's travel publications
new york · toronto · london · sydney · auckland
www.fodors.com

contents

maps

ON THE ROAD WITH FODOR'S

EVERY TRIP IS A SIGNIFICANT TRIP. Acutely aware of that fact, we've pulled out all stops in preparing Fodor's *Pocket Martha's Vineyard*. To guide you in putting together your Martha's Vineyard experience, we've created multiday itineraries and regional tours. And to direct you to the places that are truly worth your time and money, we've rallied the team of endearingly picky know-it-alls we're pleased to call our writers. Having seen all corners of Martha's Vineyard, they're real experts. If you knew them, you'd poll them for tips yourself.

Since 1970, **Perry Garfinkel** has contributed to such newspapers and magazines as *National Geographic*, *Travel & Leisure*, and *The New York Times*. The author of *Travel Writing for Profit and Pleasure*, he is also a travel expert for Trailbreaker.com. A former features editor for the *Martha's Vineyard Times*, he now teaches travel writing workshops on the Vineyard, where he happily lives, bikes, swims, plays tennis, drums, and writes.

Karl Luntta has lived on Cape Cod for a dozen years and is a frequent visitor to Martha's Vineyard. Karl has covered the Cape and islands for *Cape Cod Travel Guide*, *Cape Cod Life*, *Cape Cod Times*, and the *Hartford Courant*, among others. In addition to his published travel guides to Jamaica, St. Lucia, the Virgin Islands, and the Caribbean region, he is a frequent contributor to Fodor's *Caribbean*.

Joyce Wagner is a freelance fiction, features, travel, and column writer whose work has appeared in several Martha's Vineyard and Cape Cod magazines. She is also a former staff writer for the *Martha's Vineyard Times* and managing editor for *Planet Vineyard Magazine*. She is currently living in a log home on Cardigan Mountain in New Hampshire with her husband and two rescued greyhounds.

Don't Forget to Write

Keeping a travel guide fresh and up-to-date is a big job. So we love your feedback—positive and negative—and follow up on all suggestions. Contact the *Pocket Martha's Vineyard* editor at editors@fodors.com or c/o Fodor's, 280 Park Avenue, New York, New York 10017. And have a wonderful trip!

Karen Cure

Karen Cure

Editorial Director

martha's
vineyard

The rolling green island breaks through the haze as the ferry approaches in a light morning fog; passengers on deck begin to point and murmur, phrases breaking through the thickening summer air: "That's East Chop," someone says, and "We'll get some breakfast at the Black Dog first." But your thoughts are already on the beach, a briny day lolling in the sun, waves kissing your toes. The stuff of a reinvigorated life.

In This Chapter

By Karl Luntta

introducing martha's vineyard

FAR LESS DEVELOPED than Cape Cod—thanks to a few local conservation organizations—yet more cosmopolitan than neighboring Nantucket, Martha's Vineyard is an island with a double life. From Memorial Day through Labor Day the quieter, some might say real, Vineyard quickens into a vibrant, star-studded place. Edgartown floods with people who come to wander narrow streets flanked with elegant boutiques, stately whaling captains' homes, and charming inns. The busy main port, Vineyard Haven, welcomes day-trippers fresh off ferries and private yachts to browse in its own array of shops. Oak Bluffs, where pizza and ice cream emporiums reign supreme, attracts diverse crowds with its boardwalk-town air and nightspots that cater to high-spirited, carefree youth.

Summer regulars include a host of celebrities, among them William Styron, Art Buchwald, Walter Cronkite, Beverly Sills, Patricia Neal, Spike Lee, and Sharon Stone. President Clinton and his wife, Hillary, were frequent visitors during his terms in office. Concerts, theater, dance performances, and lecture series draw top talent to the island, while a county agricultural fair, weekly farmers' markets, and miles of walking trails provide earthier pleasures.

Most people know the Vineyard's summer persona, but in many ways its other self has even more appeal, for the off-season island is a place of peace and simple beauty. Drivers traversing country lanes through the agricultural center of the island find time to

Exploring Martha's Vineyard

The island is roughly triangular, with maximum distances of about 20 mi east to west and 10 mi north to south. The west end of the Vineyard, known as Up-Island—from the nautical expression of going "up" in degrees of longitude as you sail west—is more rural and wild than the eastern Down-Island end, comprising Vineyard Haven, Oak Bluffs, and Edgartown. Conservation land claims almost a quarter of the island, with preservationist organizations acquiring more all the time. The Land Bank, funded by a tax on real-estate transactions, is a leading group, set up to preserve as much of the island in its natural state as is possible and practical.

You might want to spend a short time in Vineyard Haven before getting rural Up-Island or heading for a beach. Or you might prefer to go straight to Edgartown to stroll past the antique white houses, pop into a museum or two, and shop. If you just want to have fun, Oak Bluffs, with its harbor scene and nearby beaches, will be the place to go. In essence, pick and choose what you like best—the Vineyard is small enough that you can pick one town as your base and explore other areas easily.

linger over pastoral and ocean vistas, without being pushed along by a throng of other cars, bicycles, and mopeds. In nature reserves, the voices of summer are gone, leaving only the sounds of birdsong and the crackle of leaves underfoot. Private beaches open to the public, and the water sparkles under crisp, blue skies.

Locals are at their convivial best off-season. After the craziness of their short moneymaking months, they reestablish contact with friends and take up pastimes temporarily crowded out by work. The result for visitors—besides the extra dose of friendliness—is that cultural, educational, and recreational events continue year-round.

THE MAKING OF MARTHA'S VINEYARD

The islands of Martha's Vineyard and Nantucket, as well as the entire Cape Cod peninsula, were formed during the slow movements of massive sheets of ice during the last great Ice Age. Starting about 2.5 million years ago, great blocks of ice, some as thick as 2 mi, descended from the frigid northern climes onto continental Europe and North America. As the ice slowly but inexorably gouged and plowed its way south, it pushed before it mounds of earth and rock. Here, in more temperate climes, and over thousands of millenniums, the glacial advance slowed. The ice began to recede some 20,000 years ago. During this period, the island, as well as Nantucket and the Elizabeth Islands, were connected to the mainland, and humans trekked to the area to establish settlements. As the ice melted, sea levels rose—some believe today's level is 400 ft higher than during glacial times—and the islands' connection to the mainland disappeared under water. Receding glaciers also gouged large holes in the earth, which in turn fused with underground springs to become the streams, bogs, and freshwater ponds found throughout the Cape and islands.

Rock debris and glacial till (sand and clay) pushed south by the great sheets of ice were left behind after the glacier retreated, forming much of the Martha's Vineyard terrain as we now know it. Throughout the island, but more pronounced along its western side, are moraines, small hills formed from glacial deposits, and great stones (Waskosim's Rock is a good example) seemingly dropped out of the sky. Also left behind were outwash plains, the flat or gently sloping surfaces most common along the island's southern and eastern coastal areas.

Theories regarding the earliest arrival of Europeans to the island are inconclusive. Some believe that the Vikings, who had established bases in today's Greenland and Newfoundland,

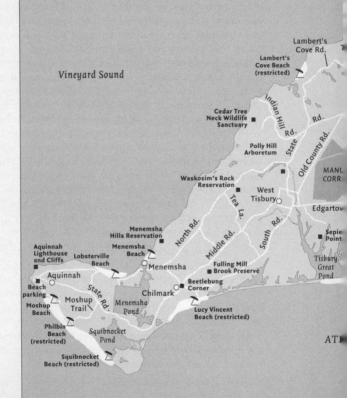

Vineyard Sound

Lambert's Cove Rd.

Lambert's Cove Beach (restricted)

Cedar Tree Neck Wildlife Sanctuary

Polly Hill Arboretum

Indian Hill Rd.

State Rd.

Old County Rd.

MANU CORR

Waskosim's Rock Reservation

West Tisbury

Edgartow

Menemsha Hills Reservation

Menemsha Beach

Menemsha

Aquinnah Lighthouse and Cliffs

Lobsterville Beach

Aquinnah

Beach parking

Moshup Beach

Moshup Trail

State Rd.

Menemsha Pond

Chilmark

North Rd.

Middle Rd.

Tea La.

South Rd.

Fulling Mill Brook Preserve

Beetlebung Corner

Lucy Vincent Beach (restricted)

Sepie Point

Tisbury Great Pond

Philbin Beach (restricted)

Squibnocket Pond

Squibnocket Beach (restricted)

AT

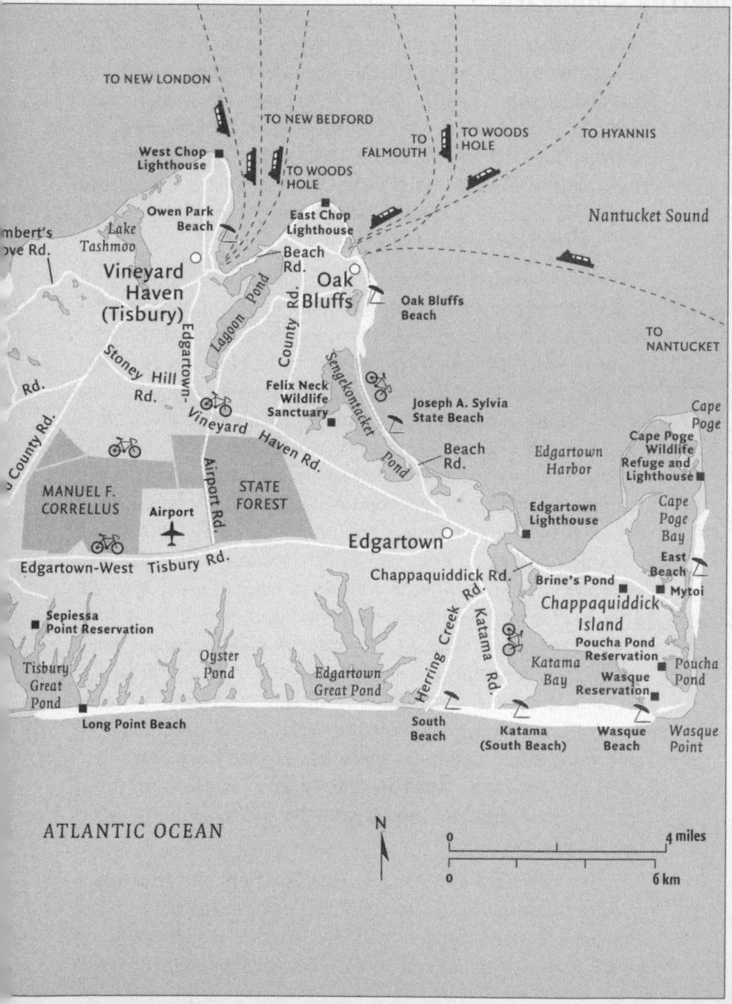
TO NEW LONDON
TO NEW BEDFORD
TO FALMOUTH
TO WOODS HOLE
TO HYANNIS
West Chop Lighthouse
TO WOODS HOLE
East Chop Lighthouse
Nantucket Sound
Owen Park Beach
Lake Tashmoo
Vineyard Haven (Tisbury)
Beach Rd.
Oak Bluffs
Oak Bluffs Beach
Lagoon Pond
County Rd.
TO NANTUCKET
Edgartown-Vineyard Haven Rd.
Stoney Hill Rd.
Rd.
County Rd.
Felix Neck Wildlife Sanctuary
Sengekontacket Pond
Joseph A. Sylvia State Beach
Beach Rd.
Edgartown Harbor
Cape Poge
Cape Poge Wildlife Refuge and Lighthouse
MANUEL F. CORRELLUS
Airport
Airport Rd.
STATE FOREST
Edgartown Lighthouse
Cape Poge Bay
Edgartown
East Beach
Edgartown-West Tisbury Rd.
Chappaquiddick Rd.
Brine's Pond
Mytoi
Chappaquiddick Island
Sepiessa Point Reservation
Herring Creek Rd.
Katama Rd.
Poucha Pond Reservation
Tisbury Great Pond
Oyster Pond
Edgartown Great Pond
Katama Bay
Wasque Reservation
Poucha Pond
Long Point Beach
South Beach
Katama (South Beach)
Wasque Beach
Wasque Point
ATLANTIC OCEAN
N
0
4 miles
0
6 km

attempted to settle the New England area some 500 years before Columbus stumbled upon the Americas but were repelled by substantive resistance by indigenous people. There is no evidence that Vikings ever arrived on Martha's Vineyard. However, in 1524 the Italian explorer Giovanni di Verrazano (the famous Verrazano-Narrows Bridge in New York is named after him), under a charter from the king of France, did chart much of the east coast of today's United States. He is credited with naming the island Louisa, although he never set foot on its shores.

Bartholomew Gosnold charted Martha's Vineyard for the British Crown in 1602 and is credited with naming it, supposedly after his infant daughter or mother-in-law (or both) and the wild grapes he found growing in profusion. Later, Massachusetts Bay Colony businessman Thomas Mayhew was given a grant to the island, along with Nantucket and the Elizabeth Islands, from King Charles of England. Mayhew's son, Thomas Jr., founded the first European settlement here in 1642 at Edgartown, finding the resident Wampanoags good neighbors. The Wampanoags called their island Noepe, thought to mean "Island in the Streams." Among other survival skills, they taught the settlers to kill whales on shore. When moved out to sea, this practice would bring the island great prosperity, for a time. Historians estimate a Wampanoag population of 3,000 upon Mayhew's arrival. Today there are approximately 300 members of the tribe living on the island, with another 600 Wampanoags living off-island. The tribe is now working hard to reclaim and perpetuate its cultural identity, and it has managed to take back nearly 500 acres of ancestral lands in the town of Aquinnah (from Acquiadene-auke, for "Land Under the Hill"), formerly called Gay Head.

Europeans settled as a community of farmers and fishermen, and both occupations continue to flourish. In the early 1800s, the basis of the island's economy made a decided shift to whaling. Never as influential as Nantucket or New Bedford,

When to Tour Martha's Vineyard

Summer is the most popular season on the Vineyard, the time when everyone is here and everything is open and happening. With weather perfect for all kinds of activities, the island hosts special events from the Martha's Vineyard Agricultural Fair to the Edgartown Regatta. Fall brings cool weather, harvest celebrations, and fishing derbies. Tivoli Day, celebrating the end of summer and the start of fall, includes a street fair. The island does tend to curl up in winter, when many shops and restaurants close. However, for the weeks surrounding the Hanukkah–Christmas–New Year's holidays, the Vineyard puts bells on for all kinds of special events and celebrations, most notably in Edgartown and Vineyard Haven. Spring sees the island awaken from its slumber in a burst of garden and house tours as islanders warm up for the busy season.

Martha's Vineyard nonetheless held its own, and many of its whaling masters returned home wealthy men. Especially during the industry's golden age, between 1830 and 1845, captains built impressive homes with their profits. These, along with many graceful houses from earlier centuries, still line the streets of Vineyard Haven and Edgartown, both former whaling towns. The industry went into decline after the Civil War, but by then revenue from tourism had picked up, and those dollars just keep flooding in.

The story of the Vineyard's development as a resort begins in 1835, when the first Methodist Camp Meeting—a two-week gathering of far-flung parishes for group worship and a healthy dose of fun—was held in the Oak Bluffs area, barely populated at the time. From the original meeting's 9 tents, the number grew to 250 by 1857. Little by little, returning campers built permanent platforms arranged around the central preachers' tent. Then the odd cottage popped up in place of a tent. By 1880, Wesleyan Grove, named for Methodism's founder, John Wesley, was a community of about 500 tiny cottages built in a hybrid of European Gothic Revival styles. Lacy filigree insets of jigsaw-cut detail work—known as gingerbread—began to appear on cottage facades, and the ornamented look came to be known as Carpenter Gothic.

Meanwhile, burgeoning numbers of cottagers coming to the island each summer helped convince speculators of its desirability as a resort destination, and in 1867 they laid out a separate secular community alongside the Camp Ground. Steamers from New Bedford, Boston, New York, and elsewhere brought in fashionable folk for bathing and taking in the sea air, for picking berries, or for playing croquet. Grand hotels sprang up around Oak Bluffs Harbor. A railroad followed, connecting the town with the beach at Katama. The Victorian seaside resort was called Cottage City before its name changed to Oak Bluffs.

More than 300 of the Camp Ground cottages remain. And just as Edgartown and Vineyard Haven reflect their origins as whaling ports, so Oak Bluffs—with its porch-wrapped beach houses and a village green where families still gather to hear the town band play in the gazebo—evokes the days of Victorian summer ease, of flowing white dresses and parasols held languidly against the sun.

ORIGINAL VINEYARDERS: THE WAMPANOAGS

For some 5,000 years before the first Europeans set foot on Martha's Vineyard, the island was inhabited by the Wampanoags, a subgroup of the larger Native American Wampanoag and

Algonquin tribes of the northeastern mainland. The Martha's Vineyard Wampanoags called the island Noepe, meaning "Dry Land amid Waters," a prescient name given their traditional endeavors of farming and fishing. The tribe had settled throughout the island but were based in the southwestern peninsula at Aquinnah, from a word meaning "Land Under the Hill," thought to be a reference to the massive Aquinnah Cliffs.

The Wampanoags were, and remain to an extent, a communal group, with an economy based on the distribution of land and goods. Their subgroups were ruled by sachems, or chiefs, organized into a confederacy of the larger Wampanoag tribes under a supreme sachem. They based many of their teachings and legends on the leader Moshup, a giant semideity possessed of great strength and power who resided in the Aquinnah Cliffs and taught his people how to fish and hunt—he was said to wade into the ocean to catch whales, dashing them against the cliffs, which explains the reddish color of their clay today. He ate entire whales and tossed the ocean behemoths ashore for his people, and today the tribal symbol of the Aquinnah Wampanoags shows Moshup on the cliffs hoisting up a great whale. Moshup legends also explain the creation of the island, as well as nearby Nantucket and the Elizabeth Islands.

In the early and mid-17th century, the island's first European colonists found the tribe accepting, if wary. The first years of settlement were marked, by most accounts, by friendly relations as the Wampanoags taught the settlers the ways of the wilderness and the English imported the modernity of Europe, which included guns for hunting, farming implements, and, unfortunately, disease. While many of the Wampanoag tribes on the mainland and Nantucket were eliminated by disease, the Martha's Vineyard tribe managed to avoid complete devastation. There were some skirmishes over land, but none so terrible as the King Philip's War of 1675–76, which saw a mainland sachem named Metacomet (dubbed King Philip by the English) rally

Wampanoag and other Native American forces to battle the accelerated European encroachment of traditional hunting and farming lands. The war was a disaster for the mainland Wampanoags, who lost thousands, including Metacomet himself. He was shot and beheaded, and his skull was placed on a pole and displayed in Plymouth for 25 years. Only 400 mainland Wampanoags remained alive after the war.

The island Wampanoags remained neutral during King Philip's War, but the result was a heightened wariness between the Native Americans and their English neighbors. For hundreds of years thereafter, the English stepped up their Christian proselytizing, turning out hundreds of "Praying Indians," as the converted were called. Evidence can today be seen in Christiantown, an area set aside by a sachem of the Takemmy area known as Josias, who created the township in 1660 for his group of Praying Indians. On the site is an ancient cemetery and the Mayhew Chapel, named after the governor and missionary Thomas Mayhew.

Between Martha's Vineyard and Nantucket, Wampanoags numbered about 700 until an unknown epidemic wiped out nearly all the Nantucket tribe. The last surviving Nantucket Wampanoag died in 1855. Wampanoags from the mainland and Cape Cod emigrated to Martha's Vineyard, adding to the numbers somewhat, but by the mid-19th century, only about 40 island tribal members were full-blooded Native Americans. Under the federal controls of the Bureau of Indian Affairs, the Wampanoags of Martha's Vineyard and the mainland banded together in 1928 to become the loosely organized Wampanoag Nation. This designation allowed for limited self government within tribal lands and was a precursor to eventual full recognition of the tribe. There are currently five bands of Wampanoags in Massachusetts, but only the Martha's Vineyard Aquinnah group has been granted federal and state recognition as a Native American tribe. Status was approved in 1987 after years of petitioning the U.S. Congress.

Along with the granting of tribal status, the Wampanoags were given back nearly 500 acres of tribal lands in the area called Gay Head. That name was changed back, by a state legislative act, to the original Wampanoag name Aquinnah in 1998. There is no true reservation at Aquinnah, but tribal headquarters are in this most rural section of the island. The Wampanoag tribe is governed by an elected Tribal Council, with traditional positions held by a chief (currently Donald Malonson) and medicine man (Luther Madison), who maintain their status for life.

While the traditions of the Wampanoags have been diluted by time and history, a resurgence of interest in the old ways has been brewing for some time. Wampanoag festivals include the recently revived Legends of Moshup Pageant, where ancient tales are reenacted using traditional dress and performances. The pageant takes place at sunset on the third Saturday in July and August, on Boyer's Hill in the Aquinnah tribal lands. Cranberry Day celebrates the traditional harvest with singing and dancing, and a potluck supper. True to their communal origins, the Wampanoags continue to take care of their own: the tribe maintains some 28 units of affordable housing for tribal members and elders and owns several island businesses. And, throughout Martha's Vineyard, the tangible reminders of the island's aboriginals remain in such place names as Chappaquiddick, Menemsha, Katama, and Takemmy.

WHALING: A MARTHA'S VINEYARD TRADITION

Whales have been good to New England—so good that, for a time from the early 18th to the mid-19th century, whale hunting and processing just about built the economic infrastructures of New Bedford, Cape Cod, Nantucket, and Martha's Vineyard. During those halcyon years, sea captains' homes were the most lavish in town, and widow's walks on rooftops became all the rage as families waited for their men to return from as long as three years at sea.

During the early 1700s, Martha's Vineyard colonists and the Native American Wampanoags alike profited from the abundance of whales offshore. Whales were so thick in the immediate area that all that was necessary to harvest them was a small boat, a harpoon, and several strong-armed men. The Wampanoags, in particular, used all parts of the whale, including its meat, oil, and bones. So important were whales to Wampanoag culture that the tribe often stipulated rights to offshore whaling and beached whales whenever they sold land to the whites. In fact, the Wampanoags, as indigenous people, to this day retain the right to claim any beached whales.

The settlers, on the other hand, were most interested in whale oil that provided fuel (often for lighthouses); spermaceti, which was used to make candles; ambergris, added to perfumes; and whale bones, which formed the ivory background for jewelry and other items.

By the 1760s, the whale population in the island waters had been depleted to the extent that small boats and crews could no longer sail far enough to capture them. This ushered in the era of large seagoing schooners and ships that sought whales as far away as the Pacific. Edgartown, with its natural and protected deep harbor, as well as Vineyard Haven became important whaling ports, though they never handled the volume of ships that docked in Nantucket and New Bedford.

Edgartown was the whaling capital of the island. Evidence of the town's wealth is seen in the stately sea captains' mansions along North and South Water streets, facing the harbor, and in Main Street's Old Whaling Church, a magnificent Greek Revival structure with immense columns. Edgartown's 1840 Fisher House, open for tours, was the home of Dr. Daniel Fisher, who built factories in town to process the whales and who was at one time the primary supplier of whale oil throughout the region.

Herman Melville, one of the whaling industry's greatest chroniclers, shipped into Edgartown on a whaler named the *Acushnet*. In his seminal 1851 novel, *Moby-Dick; or, The Whale*, an Aquinnah Wampanoag character named Tashtego is considered to be the most skillful of all harpooners.

American commercial whaling reached its peak in 1846, when 740 vessels and some 70,000 people were engaged in the industry. By the end of the 19th century, the great whaling days were over. Cheaper and easier-to-gather fuel in the form of kerosene was discovered in the process of refining crude oil, and the whale population had been decimated. Attacks by Confederate ships during the American Civil War hindered the great whaling fleets, and the industry dwindled with the onset of the Industrial Revolution. Martha's Vineyard became known more as a vacation retreat than whaling center, and the great captains' manses, once passed along through generations of family, ended up in the hands of investors and outsiders, many destined to become the B&Bs and inns so popular on the island today.

GETTING AROUND THE ISLAND

At the height of summer, Martha's Vineyard traffic can be, in a word, horrible. The island population increases a breathtaking seven-fold in summer, when thousands of cars and their passengers make the crossing weekly from Cape Cod and elsewhere and visitors by the plane and ferry load keep island roads busy with rental cars. Parking is near to impossible in Edgartown, Vineyard Haven, and Oak Bluffs, and all in all, it's the downside to vacationing on this otherwise welcoming island.

To make your life and everyone else's life easier while on the Vineyard, consider these tips for getting around:

Use public transportation whenever possible. Island shuttles and buses of the Martha's Vineyard Transit Authority circle the towns and connect them to each other, with expanded summer schedules that keep them moving as quickly as every 15 minutes and well into the night. The cost is minimal, less than $5 for most destinations, and you'll never have to worry about parking. The buses are comfortable, clean, and, in some cases, air-conditioned.

Hail a taxi. You'll never have the hassle of looking for parking or getting lost and you'll enjoy door-to-door service; however, it is more expensive. Dozens of taxi companies ply the Martha's Vineyard roads, and if you jump in a cab and enjoy the service, grab a business card and call them for pick-ups from your hotel or rental house. Most taxi companies also offer private tours.

Bike it. Martha's Vineyard has miles of accessible biking trails, some into conservation areas and parks, others safely placed parallel to major roads that link the towns, such as the Oak Bluffs–Edgartown stretch along Beach Road or the Edgartown–Vineyard Haven Road. Note there are few bike paths in Chilmark and Aquinnah, so riding on the side of the road is the only option. With a bike, you'll never have to worry about parking, and, a plus, you'll be able to access beaches where parking is restricted to sticker holders. Parking racks have been placed all around the towns and beach areas. You can bring your bike over by ferry for as little as $5 or rent a bike for a week from the many agencies listed here. Rental agencies also rent the accouterments of bike travel, such as helmets, children's seats, and tow-behinds. Remember to ride on the right in single file and follow traffic laws. In Massachusetts, children 12 and under are required to wear safety helmets, and children under 1 are not allowed to be transported on a bicycle.

Rent a moped. Mopeds are not the safest form of transport, and they're the bane of both local and visiting drivers, but they're relatively cheap (about $35 per day if you rent for a week) and can get you from one end of the island to another without a lot of effort—although at a maximum speed of just 30 mph. If you do rent one, wear a helmet, stay off the bike paths, hug the right side of the road, and follow traffic laws.

Rent a car. The simple advantage to renting? With no advance reservation to make, it's easier than bringing a car over. When using a rental, make sure you ask the agency for a good map, which should be provided free. Free maps are also available at the Chamber of Commerce in Vineyard Haven or at several information centers around the island. Better maps can be bought at Bunch of Grapes and other bookstores, as well as souvenir shops, for about $5. As well, when booking your hotel inquire about parking and beach stickers. While most of the larger hotels provide parking for guests, many of the smaller inns and B&Bs do not. Some, but not all, hotels and inns provide temporary beach stickers.

Martha's Vineyard roads are in fine shape, and you'll never need a 4WD jeep to get anywhere other than the several beaches that require Off Road Vehicle permits. If you intend to do off-road driving, note that several rental companies provide the proper stickers with the vehicle—call ahead to inquire.

Finally, if you're convinced you need your own car on Martha's Vineyard, remember that during the summer advance ferry reservations are required. The above suggestions regarding maps, hotel parking, and beach stickers apply. Be aware, also, that gasoline is several cents more per gallon than on the mainland.

THE AFRICAN AMERICAN TRADITION OF MARTHA'S VINEYARD

Martha's Vineyard's long history of African American presence has added richness to the island's culture and history. The first colonial settlers brought enslaved servants with them as early as the mid-17th century, many of whom remained on the island to work the land and the ocean as freed men. An early mention of land ownership by a person of African descent is found in the 1763 will of a Wampanoag man named Elisha Amos, who left his land to his wife, Rebecca, who was enslaved on a nearby farm. Later, the whaling industry became a major source of employment for African American men, including one William Martin, whose great-grandmother was Rebecca Amos. Martin became a whaler and ultimately a ship's captain in a career that lasted 40 years. During the years before the Civil War, spots on the island were, informally, part of the famed Underground Railroad, which sought to spirit escaped slaves to freedom in Canada and elsewhere. Later, the fishing industry attracted skilled sailors of the Cape Verde islands, a Portuguese possession off the coast of West Africa.

The evolution of the Methodist Camp Ground of Oak Bluffs (then part of Edgartown) in the mid-19th century replaced the ennui of the post–Civil War era and approaching industrial revolution with a new industry—tourism. The first tourists, propelled by the fervor of religion and by the beauty of the seaside spot, first built the town as a place of quiet retreat. It soon grew to its present status as a popular resort town, built, in great part, by the influx of African Americans of the late-19th and early 20th centuries. Attracted to its sense of community and spirit, African Americans settled in large numbers and visited in droves, and succeeding generations have carried on the tradition. Those who made the Vineyard their permanent or vacation home include the late novelist and Harlem Renaissance icon Dorothy West, as well as today's luminaries Spike Lee and Vernon Jordan.

Today's summertime island population is diverse, and the well-established African Americans and other people of color of the year-round population—the police chiefs, the inn owners, the farmers—acknowledge their history through the self-guided African American Heritage Trail. The trail highlights spots and areas on the island important to the history of all islanders and includes the homes of prominent African American islanders, the Shearer Cottage of Oak Bluffs, and spots where African Americans gathered for worship. As of this writing, trail maps were being produced.

Some information for this article was provided by Grace Lynis, managing director of Cinnamon Traveler Vineyard Tours (☞ Chapter 10).

In paradise, everything is perfect, right? Not true even on this island Eden. But even a rainy day can be turned into a day filled with memories that will shine well into the winter. All it takes is a little planning, a little flexibility, a little adventurousness, and the perfect plan.

In This Chapter

By Perry Garfinkel and Joyce Wagner

perfect days

THE PERFECT RAINY DAY

After you've assessed that gray skies and steady downpour do not constitute beach weather, start your day curled up with a good book. Lacking reading material, get up early and visit Bickerton & Ripley in Edgartown or Bunch of Grapes in Vineyard Haven, well-stocked bookstores. Book Den East, in a converted barn in Oak Bluffs, is full of rare and fascinating used books. Or drop by one of the six island libraries.

By late morning, with cabin fever setting in, visit the small handful of island museums. The Martha's Vineyard Historical Society houses exhibits in the Captain Pease House, the Gale Huntington Library of History, and the Foster Gallery—all in Edgartown. The Vincent House Museum, also in Edgartown, contains displays of early island life. While in Edgartown, have lunch at the cozy, wood-paneled Newes from America; if it's chilly, there may be a blaze in the fireplace (even in summer).

After lunch, for kids and kids-at-heart, there's the video arcade in Oak Bluffs and, across the street, the Flying Horses carousel. For adults there's the Offshore Ale brew pub, also in Oak Bluffs, where dart enthusiasts can find formidable foes.

By late afternoon and into evening, movies can distract you from the downpour. However, island theaters rarely show matinees earlier than 4 PM. If you're renting a house that has a TV and a VCR, you're set. There are great video rental shops in the Down-Island towns. Up-Island try Alley's General Store in West Tisbury and the Harbor Craft Shop in Menemsha. The libraries also have videos for overnight loan. Other than that, there's no better place than an island to stare out a window on a rainy day and daydream . . . of sunny days.

A PERFECT DAY FOR ROMANCE

One day isn't long enough for all of the activities couples can enjoy on the island, but here are a few good suggestions.

Start with a romantic breakfast. Enjoy a gourmet omelet at the historic Daggett House in Edgartown, filled with the aura of the old whaling days. Ask your waiter about the hidden staircase and the resident ghosts. If your heart is fuller than your pocketbook, Linda Jean's in Oak Bluffs is the place to hold hands and people-watch while noshing on fruit-filled pancakes.

If you're on-island on a summer Saturday, drop by the Farmer's Market in West Tisbury. Stroll from table to table and purchase a lunch of island-made jams or salsas, a loaf of bread, some fresh carrots and other snacking vegetables, and a muffin or two for dessert. Or try the Vineyard Foodshop (better known as Humphrey's Bakery) on State Road in West Tisbury, a favorite among the locals.

Once you've assembled your lunch, head for the beach. Since romance is your goal, opt for the quiet, less-populated Long Point Beach off Edgartown–West Tisbury Road. Turn on to Waldron's Bottom Road and follow the signs. In July and August, get there early; the parking lot fills up fast. Spend your day relaxing in the sun and watching the osprey dive for fish or viewing little brown crabs scooting through the water near shore. The beach closes at 5 PM, which gives you just enough time to shower, pick up a bottle of wine, and head for Menemsha. Buy carry-out lobster dinners from the back door of the popular Home Port Restaurant. Take them to the beach in Menemsha and settle onto a big rock or throw out a blanket on the sand. There's nothing more romantic than one of Menemsha's famous sunsets to complete your day.

A PERFECT HOLIDAY

Time your visit right, and a perfect holiday starts on the dock where you can greet Santa as he arrives on the morning ferry in Vineyard Haven. After you've seen Santa, you can shop along the town's Main Street: one of the best perks of being on the Vineyard during the holidays is the peaceful and relaxed pace of shopping as compared to the frenetic mainland. Keep an eye out for holiday fairs and bazaars, sponsored by local groups and benefiting island charities, where island-made crafts are featured. Continue in the shopping mode along Circuit Avenue in Oak Bluffs and Main Street in Edgartown. In both towns many of the island's best inns and B&Bs don their gayest apparel over the holidays and open their doors for tours; check the papers for times and dates and make sure to visit a few for a quick peek and a glass of cider.

In the afternoon, though it may be a bit nippy, revive yourself with a brisk walk on any of the island's town or private beaches. Or, check with the Felix Neck Wildlife Sanctuary for seasonal guided nature walks. In the early evening, treat yourself to a festive meal. Dressed in holiday lights and colors, the Coach House at the Harbor View Hotel in Edgartown is a lovely, traditional setting for a holiday dinner. Come evening, catch a holiday show at the Vineyard Playhouse in Vineyard Haven. Past performances have included "The Snow Queen," "A Christmas Carol," and "A Christmas for Jennie." Or attend a holiday concert by the highly regarded Martha's Vineyard Regional High School singing group, the Minnesingers, or the Island Community Chorus's rendition of Handel's *Messiah*. For a late repast, a nibble from the bar menu at Atria or Alchemy, both in Edgartown, washed down with some warm holiday drinks, is the perfect way to end the day and fill your holiday heart.

You're basking on a beach, not a care in the world, and suddenly the rumblings in your stomach drown out the crash of the waves. A riveting question breaks your meditative haze: "Where shall we eat?" Quick bites, fine dining, casual bistros, family fare: the answers are nearly infinite on Martha's Vineyard.

In This Chapter

By Perry Garfinkel

dining

FROM FRIED FISH AT ROAD-SIDE STANDS to foie gras at fancy French restaurants, from standard New England fare—clam chowder and boiled lobster—to a growing array of international influences—Thai, Venezuelan, Japanese, Mexican, to name just a few—the Vineyard offers an amazing variety of culinary choices. In addition, due to the influence of islanders of Portuguese descent, you'll find such Portuguese home-style dishes as kale soup and linguiça (a garlic-spiced sausage) on many menus. The majority of eating establishments, both take-out and sit-down, are concentrated in the three Down-Island towns of Vineyard Haven, Oak Bluffs, and Edgartown. As you travel Up-Island—to West Tisbury, Chilmark, and Aquinnah—choices dwindle, especially when it comes to sit-down dinners.

Sadly, Vineyard diners—all-American institutions where you can get an honest, no-frills meal at reasonable prices—are a dying breed. Notable for their willingness to serve simple but good dishes such as bacon and eggs with home fries or meat loaf or tuna melt are the Main Street Diner in Edgartown, Linda Jean's in Oak Bluffs, and the ArtCliff in Vineyard Haven. Luckily, there are a number of places around the island where you can pick up a sandwich or pastry and other to-go specialties and with good planning you can eat well on a modest budget and splurge for an elegant dinner.

Part of how the Vineyard maintains its charm—and part of what makes it somewhat frustrating as well—is that alcoholic beverages are sold in retail stores and in restaurants in only two towns, Edgartown and Oak Bluffs. At restaurants in the so-called "dry" towns of Vineyard Haven, West Tisbury, Chilmark, and Aquinnah you can BYOB, but only if you've had the foresight to visit a "wet" town for provisions first. Also, once at the restaurant, expect to be charged up to $5 for corkage fees (this includes the opening of the bottle and the use of glasses).

As for a general recommendation on what to order, you don't have to be a graduate of a culinary institute to realize that on an island fish is a smart bet. However, keep in mind that all fish on the menu won't have come from waters surrounding the Vineyard. Some of the more exotic species—monkfish, for example—are shipped in and fresh frozen. Ask your waiter which fish is caught locally. Bluefish, striped bass, swordfish, bay scallops—each has its own season—are among the local hauls. For those who like to cook their own, the local retail fish shops—Edgartown Seafood Market, John's and the Net Result in Vineyard Haven, and Larsen's and Poole's on the docks in Menemsha—will guide you to the fresh catches of the day, and the counter people will usually recommend their favorite recipes.

Prices

You can find places to eat at almost every price point, though increasing food costs seem to inch up the menu prices every year. You'll end up with dinner bills that run the gamut from budget to pricey—with more at the top end.

CATEGORY	COST*
$$$$	over $40
$$$	$25–$40
$$	$15–$25
$	under $15

*per person for a three-course meal, excluding drinks, service, and 5% sales tax

How and When

Most restaurants begin to open for the season in late spring, with weekend openings. By Memorial Day weekend, most eateries are open daily. While the season seems to stretch longer each season, most remain open full time through Columbus Day weekend, then only weekends through Thanksgiving. There's one last hurrah through the holiday season, and then most restaurants close until spring again. There are, however, a small handful of die-hard restaurants that stay open year-round. Dress, even for the upscale spots, is casual. A man in a sport jacket is a rare sight. Reservations are highly recommended in the summer months; you'll find some people make reservations at their favorite restaurants weeks ahead of time. Dinner reservations are more easily secured for the earlier hours.

DOWN-ISLAND

VINEYARD HAVEN (TISBURY)

$$$–$$$$ **LE GRENIER.** Up narrow stairs, above the M.V. Bagel Authority at the upper end of Vineyard Haven's downtown, owner-chef Jean Dupon has been serving classic French food since the late 1970s. While some island restaurants have come and gone, and others shifted with the newest trends, Dupon has been consistently loyal to the French standards: frogs' legs, sweetbreads, tournedos, calves' brains—26 entrées in all. His clientele have been loyal as well. They enjoy that the decor is hardly stuffy in the French tradition; rather, it's almost backyard casual, with a string of lightbulbs and souvenir wine-bottle corks lining the walls. Open year-round, in winter Le Grenier features fondue specials, including a don't-miss chocolate fondue dessert. *Upper Main St., tel. 508/693–4906. AE, MC, V. BYOB. No lunch.*

$$$–$$$$ **ZEPHRUS.** Vineyard Haven's newest entry in the restaurant feeding frenzy represents a move by Joe DaSilva, former chef at the Stand

vineyard haven dining

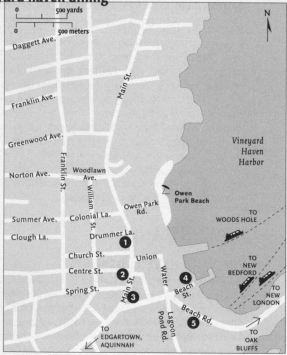

By in Oak Bluffs, to the former Tisbury Inn Cafe, next door to the Tisbury Inn (☞ Chapter 9). Owners Sherman and Susan Goldstein gutted the formerly dark space and turned it into a lively and exciting environment, with fanciful design touches (check out the handmade paper lamps in purple, blue, and yellow hanging from the ceiling). DaSilva and the crew he brought with him from Oak Bluffs prepare simple great cuisine but with panache. Cioppino (fish stew) with littleneck clams, monkfish, and shrimp in a tomato saffron broth is divine. A so-called "Cowboy Steak"—bone-in sirloin with diced root vegetables, grilled asparagus, and sun-dried cherry and port wine reduction—is bold in taste, though almost over the top. A chef's table across from the open kitchen lets you watch the kitchen artists in action. *Main St., tel. 508/693–3416. AE, MC, V. BYOB. No lunch.*

$$$ BLACK DOG TAVERN. Almost overshadowed by the success of retail sales of Black Dog T-shirts and mugs, this tavern right on the harborside, just steps from the ferry terminal in Vineyard Haven, remains a hangout for year-rounders in winter (when the lines aren't a mile long). In summer early (and we mean early) breakfast is the best bet for beating the lines; by 8 AM or so in July and August the wait can be as much as an hour. Why? Partly because the ambience inside—roaring fireplace, dark wood walls, maritime memorabilia, and a grand view of the water—makes diners feel at home, as it has since its founding in 1971. But the food is the other draw: the menu is heavy on local fish, chowders, and burgers. Breakfast is the best, winning points for perhaps the largest assortment of omelettes (with goofy island names) of any restaurant on the island. In winter, weekly theme nights—Thai, Chinese, even an Elvis Night—ward off the boredom. The bakery on Water Street and the café-bakery farther Up-Island on State Road in Vineyard Haven still make healthy breads; buy a loaf the day you leave and munch it all the way back to the mainland. *Beach St. Ext., tel. 508/693–9223. Reservations not accepted. AE, D, MC, V. BYOB. No smoking.*

$$ CAFE MOXIE. Open year-round, this classy restaurant has a handsome wooden bar (though it's a dry town) and island artists' work on the walls. Chef Merrick Kappel, originally from Canada, has come into her own with lively interpretations of New England fare. An appetizer of crispy calamari with chopped tomato salad and an avocado scallion cream is a good example. So, too, are entrées of grilled salmon with corn crusted artichokes and an herb sauce and roasted Cornish hen with mustard glaze and seasoned bread crumbs. If you stick to the creative gourmet pizzas and salads, you can actually eat here for about $20. The restaurant is across the street from the movie theater; if you're trying to make the previews, let your server know. *Main St. at Centre St., tel. 508/693–1484. D, MC, V. BYOB. Closed Mon. No lunch.*

$ ARTCLIFF. Once known to islanders for its early morning breakfasts and grand, greasy-spoon tradition (and that's meant in a good way), the ArtCliff went through a change of management in 1999 that brought new blood into the kitchen. Now Regina Stanley, who came from the Blair House in Washington, D.C., the official residence for guests of the White House, has upgraded the menu with such morning treats as frittatas, almond-crusted French toast, and buttermilk waffles and pancakes. Lunch has also been spiffed up with, among others, grilled chorizo roll and "Penne from Heaven" (cold pasta salad with crumbled feta, tomatoes, kalamata olives, and a splash of lemon and olive oil). The diner tradition is not dead; it's just gotten a welcome face-lift. *39 Beach Rd., tel. 508/693–1224. Credit cards not accepted. BYOB. No dinner.*

OAK BLUFFS

$$$–$$$$ ★ SWEET LIFE CAFÉ. Housed in a charming Victorian house, this island favorite, with its warm tones, low lighting, and handsome antique furniture, will make you feel like you've entered someone's home, but the cooking is more sophisticated than home-style. Owners Jackson and Mary Kenworth, he the chef and she the front-of-house hostess, add their very personable welcoming

The Mighty Clam

A clam is a clam—or is it? If you're confused by the names of our mollusk friends on the menu at the chowder house, then take a look at this quick clam primer, a guide to local shellfish: A **quahog** (pronounced ko-hog, derived from a Native American word) is a hard-shell clam, native in coastal areas from the Gulf of St. Lawrence to the Gulf of Mexico. Not a deep burrower, it is often found lying along the ocean bottom in relatively shallow coastal waters, just under the low-tide mark. For this reason, the clam is often harvested by using a special rake to scrape the ocean floor during low tide. The quahog gets as big as your fist, with a thickened shell in the middle. Due to their fleshy and tough body, large quahogs are often used for chowder. Small quahogs are called **littleneck** clams, and medium quahogs are called **cherrystones.** These younger and more tender versions are usually eaten raw, accompanied by wedges of lemon and various sauces.

A **steamer,** or soft-shell clam, has an elongated shell and flattened middle section. This clam is a burrower and is found in intercoastal soft sand and tidal marshes at low tide—many locals say the best time to go clamming is two to three hours after high tide. Look for a tiny hole in the sand, where the clam's elongated "neck," or siphon, waits to feed on passing microscopic marine life. Special rakes with elongated tines are used to dig under the sand, where the clams are found some 6 to 12 inches down. Steamers are tender and are usually prepared—no surprise here—by steaming them in a pot. They're served in the shell, accompanied by the water left over from steaming—which you use to rinse the flesh—and with melted butter. Steamers are also deep fried or served in chowders.

Another type of local clam is called the **surf clam** or **sea clam.** Found in deep ocean waters, this is not your recreational clammer's quarry. The large and tough clam is sought by commercial clammers, who sell it for cutting and processing as canned clams or those frozen clam strips found in supermarkets.

—By Karl Luntta

oak bluffs dining

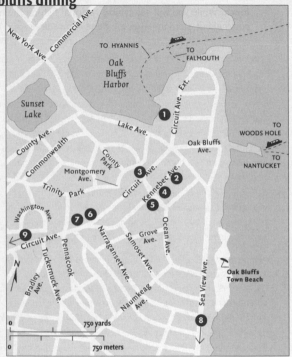

touch. While you will see typical regional fish on the menu—cod, halibut, salmon—they are done in inventive ways. The cod is served Basque style, with chorizo, peppers, onion, and local clams. The halibut comes with eggplant purée, and curried onion rings. Ratatouille Provençal, a vegetable stew, will take you to the south of France. The desserts remain superb; try the warm chocolate fondant (a sort of soufflé) with toasted almond ice cream. There's outdoor dining by candlelight in a shrub-enclosed garden, with heaters for when it turns cold. *Upper Circuit Ave., at the far end of town, tel. 508/696–0200. Reservations essential. AE, D, MC, V. Closed Jan.–Mar.*

$$$–$$$$ **BALANCE.** Owner-chef Ben deForest, who turned the Red Cat in
★ West Tisbury into a destination restaurant, opened Balance in 1999 with a bang: his buddy, summer Vineyarder and well-known actor Dan Aykroyd, rode up on a Harley. To match deForest's living-large style, the room is big and boisterous and the tastes are bold. Fish cakes are encrusted in *panko* (fine Japanese bread crumbs) with a curry emulsion for an appetizer. He turns codfish into a journey to Italy: it comes with kalamata olives, Tuscan couscous, and tarragon-infused lobster stock. Roasted loin of venison is served with creamy polenta, black mission figs, and truffled carrot purée. Bar None, a menu available only in the bar area, is available until midnight. For under $10 you can have littleneck clams with salsa and fried tortillas, chicken nuggets with chutney, or more traditional choices such as a grilled sirloin burger or baby back ribs. *57 Circuit Ave., tel. 508/696–3000. AE, D, MC, V. Closed Columbus Day–Memorial Day weekend.*

$$$–$$$$ **LOLA'S.** Boisterous and open 364 days a year (closed only on Christmas), this spot draws a party crowd. On one side is a lively bar where bands play. There's also an enclosed patio for dining and a large separate dining room on another side. In summer, with private parties in outdoor tents surrounding the restaurant, it's like a three-ring circus. The menu features Louisiana standards such as jambalaya, but there are also ribs and other standard fare. Sunday mornings bring an all-you-can-eat buffet. Be warned: this is more of a scene than a relaxing dining spot. However, the bar is big and welcoming, the wall mural is full of familiar local faces, and year-round residents appreciate the hot music in the cold of winter. *Beach Rd., just over 1 mi from Oak Bluffs, tel. 508/693–5007. D, MC, V.*

$$$–$$$$ TSUNAMI. In a quaint converted gingerbread house overlooking ★ the harbor, this restaurant has an exclusively Asian-influenced menu, a news-making rarity for the island. Chef Armand Poghosian focuses on Thai flavors but also samples from Japan, China, Burma, and other parts of Indonesia. The small upstairs dining room is decorated with a minimalist's touch; downstairs is a handsome mahogany bar along with several small tables, a fun place for casual dining, shared with the overflow of young bar patrons. The full dinner menu, which includes sushi and sake, is available on both levels. The smoky flavored lobster Rangoon, bits of meat and claw over a flaky pastry, is topped with a purée of cream cheese, walnuts, pecans, and brown sugar resulting in a richly flavorful, highly inventive dish. The tender smoked lemongrass duck is marinated in a rich and complex soy-based sauce; it's excellent. The grilled tuna, with shiitake mushrooms in a fig soy glaze, is equally successful. All the spring-roll appetizers (vegetable, mango and crab, tuna and avocado) are delicate and subtle. *6 Circuit Ave., tel. 508/696–8900. AE, MC, V. Closed Columbus Day–mid-May.*

$$–$$$ OFFSHORE ALE COMPANY. Since opening in 1997, the island's first and only microbrewery restaurant has become quite popular. There are private wooden booths, dark wood throughout, a dart board in the corner, and live music throughout the year (Wednesday-night Irish music jams are a hoot). Take your own peanuts from a barrel by the door and drop the shells on the floor; then order from a menu that includes steaks and burgers, chicken, gumbo, and fish. However, to truly appreciate the beer, try it with one of the wood-fired brick-oven pizzas. *30 Kennebec Ave., tel. 508/693–2626. Reservations not accepted. AE, MC, V.*

\$\$–\$\$\$ SMOKE 'N BONES. This is the island's only rib joint with its own smoker out back and hickory, apple, oak, and mesquite wood stacked up around the lot. The place has a cookie-cutter, prefab feeling, with all the appropriate touches like neon flames around the kitchen and marble bones for doorknobs. If you're a true ribs aficionado from the South, this may not satisfy you, but on the Vineyard it's an offbeat treat. *Siloam Rd., about 7 blocks from Oak Bluffs, tel. 508/696–7427. Reservations not accepted. MC, V.*

\$\$ JIMMY SEA'S. The irresistible fragrance of sautéed garlic wafting out its doors beckons lovers of the stinking rose. Most dishes come in the pan they're cooked in and are among the biggest portions you'll find on the island. Classic Italian dishes include *vongole* (whole littleneck clams) marinara, and linguine *puttanesca* (spicy tomato sauce with capers, olives, and anchovies). A brightly colored porch and painted ceilings add to the charm of the place. *32 Kennebec Ave., tel. 508/696–8550. Reservations not accepted. MC, V.*

\$\$ ZAPOTEC CAFE. Southwest meets gingerbread at one of the island's most unpretentious, and its only Mexican, restaurant. The crowded quarters, dressed in warm Caribbean and fruit colors and strung with chili-pepper Christmas lights, add to its character. On the menu are original versions of classic Mexican-American fare. *Tacos de pescado* lays barbecued swordfish over a creamy yogurt sauce in soft flour tortillas. Don't pass up the outstanding mussels Oaxaca, a big bowlful steamed with wine, chipotle peppers, lime, cilantro, and cream. *Kennebec Ave., tel. 508/693–6800. Reservations not accepted. AE, MC, V. Closed mid-fall–mid-spring; call for exact months.*

\$–\$\$ LINDA JEAN'S. This is a classic local hangout, a diner the way diners
★ should be: hearty helpings, inexpensive prices. Want breakfast at 6 AM? No problem. Want breakfast at 11:30 AM? No problem. Tired of the gourmet world and want comfortable booths, friendly waitresses, and few frills? No problem. The only problem: you may have to wait—even at 6 AM. *34 Circuit Ave., tel. 508/693–4093. Reservations not accepted. No credit cards.*

EDGARTOWN

$$$$ **L'ÉTOILE.** Perhaps the Vineyard's finest traditional French
★ restaurant, L'étoile carries on a long history of excellent dining.
Both the food and the setting in the stunningly appointed Charlotte
Inn (☞ Chapter 9) are unforgettable. The glass-enclosed dining
room reminds you why hunter green, dark wood, and glass
became so popular—and imitated. Preparations are at once
classic and creative. Not to be missed are a terrine of grilled
vegetable appetizer, roasted ivory king salmon with a wonderful
horseradish and scallion crust, and Black Angus sirloin with
zinfandel and oyster sauce. The outstanding wine list has selections
from California and Europe that are solid, if a little pricey. During
the shoulder seasons (May–mid-June, September) the restaurant's
weekday schedule varies. 27 S. Summer St., tel. 508/627–5187.
Reservations essential. AE, MC, V. Closed Jan.–mid-Feb. and weekdays Oct.–
Dec. and late Feb.–Apr. No lunch.

$$$$ **SAVOIR FARE.** With guests from Walter Cronkite to William Styron
★ to Bill Clinton, Savoir Fare has carved out a reputation as the
Vineyard's celebrity favorite. At first glance there's no obvious
reason: the big black-and-white diamonds painted on the wood
floor are nice but not so special, the buff walls and gauzy white
linen can be found everywhere, and even the view of the small
garden and patio is island typical. What is it, then? The food!
"Summer on a Plate" presents roasted striped bass with ripe
peach and tomato jelly, grilled Vidalia onion and basil salad, and
handmade potato chips. You can be sure the fish and meat are
top quality, but "Salad Like the Chefs Eat" (hot potato salad and
cold iceberg lettuce with "salad bar vegetables") is a cute concept
that shouldn't cost $9.50. 14 Church St., in courtyard opposite Main
St.'s town hall, tel. 508/627–9864. Reservations essential. AE, MC, V. Closed
Nov.–Apr. No lunch.

$$$–$$$$ **ALCHEMY BISTRO AND BAR.** According to the menu, the
dictionary meaning of *alchemy* is "a magic power having as its
asserted aim the discovery of a panacea and the preparation of

the elixir of longevity"—lofty goals for yet another French-style bistro. This high-class version has elegant gray wainscoting, classic paper-covered white tablecloths, old wooden floors, and an opening cut into the ceiling to reveal the second-floor tables. The only things missing are the patina of age, experience, cigarette smoke—and French working folk's prices. The same people own Savoir Fare (☞ *above*), so you can expect quality and imagination. One example is a cumin-crusted halibut with roasted yucca and watercress. The alcohol list, long and complete, includes cognacs, grappas, and beers. *71 Main St., tel. 508/627–9999. AE, MC, V.*

$–$$ LATTANZI'S PIZZERIA. Albert and Cathy Lattanzi's big brick oven gets fired up by 2:30 PM, and the pizza that slides out come evening is delicious—baby clams with plum tomatoes, oregano, spinach, roasted garlic, and Asiago cheese is just one example. A Tuscan landscape mural with Bacchus presiding over his harvest circles the walls; you'll be able to salute him year-round. *Old Post Office Sq., tel. 508/627–9084. AE, D, DC, MC, V. No lunch.*

$–$$ NEWES FROM AMERICA. Sometimes a nearly subterranean, darkened scene feels right on a hot summer afternoon, in which case the Newes is the perfect spot for an informal lunch or dinner. Inside, there's plenty of wood and greenery and many things "olde." The food is mostly Americana (burgers and fries), though some dishes like "Roquefort Stilettos" (French bread, Roquefort cheese, and bacon) have made their way onto the menu. There's a massively inclusive list of microbrew beers, and the staff is well equipped to make recommendations. The Newes is open from 11 AM until midnight every day of the year except Christmas. *23 Kelly St., tel. 508/627–4397. Reservations not accepted. AE, D, MC, V.*

$ EDGARTOWN DELI. A no-frills place with a down-home, happy feeling, this deli has walls and a glass counter plastered with specials written on multicolored paper. Brightly lighted booths fill one side of the room, while customers line up at the counter for orders to go. Breakfast specials are served from 8 until 10:45

edgartown dining

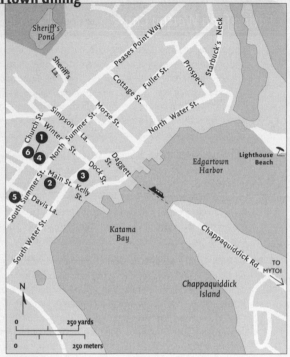

Eating for a Worthy Cause

Vineyarders love to eat and they love to raise funds for worthy causes. So what better way to accomplish both than with benefit food events? Visitors with appetites and altruistic tendencies are always invited. Among the smorgasbord of annual possibilities is the **Taste of the Vineyard,** held in June at the Daniel Fisher House in Edgartown, which showcases some 75 local restaurants, all of which serve samples. The foodfest is a benefit for the Martha's Vineyard Preservation Trust, which acquires and preserves island buildings of historical note. tel. 508/627–4440. Tickets are $100.

At **Sail Martha's Vineyard Seafood Buffet and Auction,** held in July each year at Tisbury Wharf overlooking Vineyard Haven Harbor, there's an open raw bar, a buffet dinner, and an auction that raises funds for Sail M.V., the island's nonprofit program that promotes the long sailing tradition here. On display are a number of wooden schooners that anchor in the town harbor. tel. 508/696–7644. Tickets are $75.

The **Portuguese-American Feast,** held the third weekend in July, is a weekend event that includes dance, music, and authentic Portuguese cooking. Held at the Portuguese-American Club's building in Oak Bluffs, it raises funds that the group donates to various island charities and student scholarships. tel. 508/693–9875. Admission is free.

The **Chili Contest,** a winter event held at the Atlantic Connection, a bar in Oak Bluffs, is a benefit for the Red Stocking Fund, which provides clothing and food for needy island children at Christmas. Cosponsored by WMVY, the island radio station, it attracts contestants—and chili lovers—from throughout New England. tel. 508/693–5000. Tickets are $12.

The **Chowder Contest,** a fall event held at the Tisbury Inn in Vineyard Haven, is also a benefit for the Red Stocking Fund and is co-sponsored by WMVY. Island amateur- and pro-chefs compete in a number of categories. tel. 508/693–5000. Tickets are $12.

and feature egg, cheese, and linguiça (garlicky Portuguese sausage) on a roll. Lunch sandwiches include corned beef and Swiss, roast beef, turkey, pastrami, or steak and cheese. *52 Main St., tel. 508/ 627–4789. Reservations not accepted. No credit cards. Closed Nov.– Apr. No dinner.*

UP-ISLAND

WEST TISBURY

$$$–$$$$ ★ **LAMBERT'S COVE COUNTRY INN.** A narrow road winds through pine woods to this restaurant nestled in secluded Lambert's Cove (☞ Chapter 9). The decor of the dining room is quintessential country inn: flowered wallpaper, high-backed wooden Queen Anne chairs, doilies, fresh flowers, and a candle at each table. The innkeepers need only the slightest excuse to ignite the wood in the fireplace, adding to the room's golden glow. It's not surprising that this has been named Most Romantic Dining Spot by readers of *Cape Cod Life* for several years. As for the fare, it's classic New England with original spins. A corn soup comprises whole kernels of corn and chunks of sausage swimming in a nicely textured base. The crab cakes have a delicate shellfish taste; a key-lime mango sauce is an inspired touch. Among entrées, the honey-orange– glazed grilled duck breast is all you hope of duck: gamey but not too salty, buttery but chewy. The bed of caramelized onions and green apple chutney takes the dish to yet a higher level. Buttery-smooth rack of lamb, imported from Australia, is mint-infused and wrapped in a walnut crust and at $32, the most expensive entrée. *Off Lambert's Cove Rd., tel. 508/693–2298, fax 508/693–7890. Reservations essential. AE, MC, V. BYOB.*

CHILMARK

$$$–$$$$ **THE FEAST OF CHILMARK.** The best thing about the Feast is that it serves a reliable dinner in Chilmark, the only restaurant in the area other than the Home Port. Civilized, calm, and calming, the

Feast is a welcome break from the Down-Island eating scene. Photographer Peter Simon's work adds to the ambience in the bright and airy dining room, where the clientele is generally laid-back. Lots of seafood interpretations, light appetizers, and fresh salads play up summer tastes and flavors. For starters, try oven-seared scallops with spinach and casino butter. A fine main course is a grilled swordfish steak with cilantro lime butter. The whole menu takes advantage of local produce, and the mixed green salad is simple and perfect. *Beetlebung Corner, tel. 508/645–3553. AE, MC, V. BYOB. No lunch.*

$$$–$$$$ **BEACH PLUM INN.** A devastating fire destroyed the main building
★   (including the restaurant) of the Beach Plum Inn, but owner Craig Arnold and chef James McDonough used this unfortunate incident as an opportunity to spiff up the surroundings and the menu. New on the menu are entrées such as grilled chicken breast with crab dumplings and soybeans in a lemongrass broth; grilled sirloin atop marinated Portobello mushrooms served with Merlot mashed potatoes with haricot verts and smoked applewood bacon; and roasted whole black bass with baby leeks and Asian pears in a Pernod shrimp fumé. Still on the menu is a Beach Plum favorite, beef Wellington. The menu rotates on a weekly basis. The one entrée available every night is lobster, either steamed or grilled with caviar cream sauce. A four-course prix fixe is available for $65. *Off North Rd., tel. 508/645–9454. AE, MC, V. BYOB. No lunch.*

MENEMSHA

$$$ **HOME PORT.** An institution overlooking Menemsha Pond, the Home Port is a longtime favorite because, well, because it's been a favorite for so long. Families who return here year after year do so more out of tradition than for an incredible meal. To be sure, the fish is fresh and simply prepared, and the servings are ample. The knotty-pine walls and the fishing nets and other nautical wall hangings bring you back to a bygone era. That, too, is part of the appeal. Chef-owner Will Holtham threatened to sell the

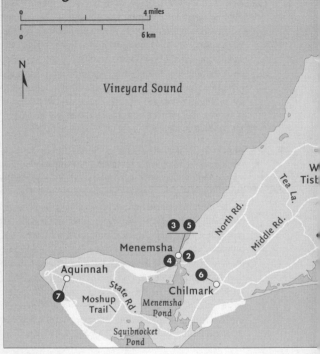

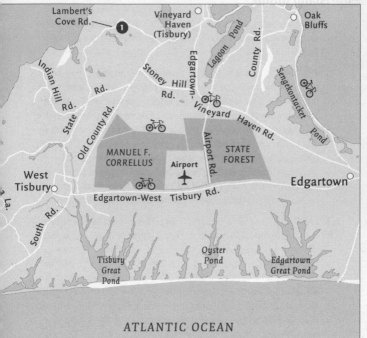

restaurant in 2000, and there was practically a revolt by loyalists; however, Holtham assures fans that he's going nowhere for quite some time. *At the end of North Rd., tel. 508/645–2679. Reservations essential. MC, V. BYOB. Closed mid-Oct.–mid-Apr. No lunch.*

$ THE BITE. Fried everything—clams, fish-and-chips, you name it—is on the menu at this simple, roadside shack, where two outdoor picnic tables are the only seating options. Small, medium, and large are the three options: all of them are perfect if you're craving that classic seaside fried lunch. But don't come on a rainy day, unless you want to get wet. A not-so-well-kept secret, the lines here can be long. To beat the crowds, try arriving between traditional mealtimes. The best advice, however, is be patient and don't arrive too hungry. The Bite closes at 3 PM weekdays, 7 PM weekends. *Basin Rd., no phone. No credit cards. Closed Oct.–late-Mar.*

$ LARSEN'S. Basically a retail fish store, Larsen's also has a raw take-out counter and will boil lobsters for you as well. A plate of fresh littlenecks or cherrystones goes for $7.50 a dozen. Oysters at a buck apiece are not a bad alternative. There's also seafood chowder and a variety of smoked fish and dips. Bring your own bottle of wine or beer, buy your dinner here, and then set up on the rocks, on the docks, or at the beach: there's no finer alfresco rustic dining on the island. Larsen's closes at 6 PM weekdays, 7 PM weekends. *Dutcher's Dock, tel. 508/645–2680. MC, V. BYOB. Closed mid-Oct.–mid-May.*

AQUINNAH

$$–$$$ THE AQUINNAH SHOP. At the far end of the row of fast-food take-out spots and souvenir shops at the Gay Head Cliffs is this restaurant owned and operated by members of the Vanderhoop and Madison families, native Wampanoags. The family took back the lease in 2000 after a four-year hiatus. Now, with chefs Marvin Jones, David Vanderhoop, Anne Vanderhoop, and Luther Madison back at the helm, the Aquinnah Shop has regained its reputation as a homey place to eat and a sort of community center for way–

Up-Islanders. For breakfast try the Tomahawk Special, two homemade fish cakes covered with salsa on top of poached eggs with melted cheddar cheese. Native American blue corn flour, which has a grainy you're-eating-something-from-the-earth natural taste, is used for Belgian waffles and pancakes. For lunch, while there are all kinds of sandwiches, burgers, and dogs, plus some healthy-sounding salads, there is really no choice but fried shellfish. Some old favorites are back for dinner: "Aquinnah by the Sea," sautéed shrimp, scallops, and lobster with rotini in a béarnaise sauce; and "Aquinnah by Land," buffalo short ribs braised in cabernet wine. The home-baked pies are well known beyond these shores: banana cream, pecan, or fruit pies (alone or in combination), wrapped in a crust so moist and flaky you want to rest your head in its lap. *State Rd., tel. 508/645–3142. MC, V. Closed mid-Oct.–mid-Apr.*

The Power Shopper leans on the forward rail of the Islander, watching the white clapboard and grey shingled buildings of Vineyard Haven grow larger in her view. Within 15 minutes she'll disembark onto her Mecca, a land of shops laden with wampum jewelry, Nantucket baskets, beach plum jam, one of a kind apparel, and marine antiques. In the tote bag hanging off her shoulder, she's packed cash, check book, her holiday gift list, and a change of shoes. Her credit card fingers are getting itchy just watching the shoreline approach. When the boat lands, she'll make a beeline for Main Street and travel up the hill on one side and down the next, stopping at every shop. In the ensuing days, she'll visit Edgartown and Oak Bluffs, then squeeze in some sightseeing while she shops the rows of shack-like stores in Menemsha and Aquinnah. Throughout her trip her mantra will continue to ring in her head, "So many shops, so little time."

In This Chapter

By Joyce Wagner

shopping

MARTHA'S VINEYARD IS A SHOPPER'S PARADISE, with a plethora of unique shops lining picturesque streets and nary a chain store or a Gap in sight (strict zoning laws make this possible). The three main towns have the largest concentrations of shops: in Vineyard Haven, most of the stores line Main Street; Edgartown's stores are clustered together within a few blocks of the dock, on Main, Summer, and Water streets; and casual clothing and gift shops crowd along Circuit Avenue in Oak Bluffs. At the Aquinnah Cliffs, touristy Native American crafts and souvenirs abound during the season, and cottage industries and the odd shop or gallery appear off the main roads in many locations.

When and How

Bring your charge cards—almost all the shops accept them. During the season, most in-town shops are open till 10 PM daily to take advantage of late-arriving visitors. Many shops will ship your items home, which is a good thing, because if you're departing on one of the dinky planes that service the island, you may have to buy a seat for that large porcelain vase you just couldn't pass up. Many Vineyard shops close for the winter, although most, especially gift shops, remain open through Christmas. If you're here in August and September, you'll find great bargains, as many of the shops that close for the winter will be shedding their inventories. Quite a few shops in Vineyard Haven and some stores in other locations remain open year-round. A call ahead saves a wasted trip.

Taking Home a Bit of Martha's Vineyard

Vineyard artists and artisans cordially invite you to leave the island—with a bit of island history. Formerly used by the Wampanoags as currency, wampum—beads made from white shells streaked with purple and fashioned into jewelry—is produced by several locals. Although the materials can be obtained on a walk on the beach, quality wampum is very expensive, since it's labor intensive to produce. The beads are hand-carved and sanded to the desired shape and design. You'll find locally produced wampum jewelry in shops throughout the island. Antique and new scrimshaw, jewelry in which a design is created by etching ink into whale ivory, is also very popular. Look for island-specific designs such as lighthouses or bunches of grapes. Many island shops carry the ultraexpensive Nantucket lightship baskets, tightly woven creations of wood and rattan that were originally made by sailors but are now valued collectibles made by artisans. Jewelry made from sea glass, although without historic significance, is becoming very popular. Grab it up while you can, since availability of authentic ocean-produced gems may ebb as its popularity swells.

For a piece of island history that comes without a costly price tag, try the beach plum, wild grape, and Russian olive jams and jellies that line the shelves of food markets and souvenir shops throughout the island. The latter is not an olive at all but a tart, amber-colored berry that grows wild on the Vineyard. The jelly is a little hard to find because, being wild, the berry is subject to the vagaries of the island's weather, but the sweet-tart flavor is well worth the search. Beach plums love the island's sandy soil, but if the price tag for a jar of jelly or jam seems a little steep, it's because gatherers must brave fields of poison ivy to collect the fruit. Perhaps Mother Nature isn't as generous as the island artisans in hoping you take a piece of the island home.

DOWN-ISLAND

VINEYARD HAVEN (TISBURY)
Antiques

A. E. Kirkpatrick (30 Main St., inside Amelia Bloomers, tel. 508/693–1632) carries vintage and estate jewelry and a wide array of compacts and cigarette cases. It also deals in contemporary wampum and sea-glass jewelry

Gone with the Wind (18 Main St., tel. 508/696–8522) specializes in vintage and estate jewelry, beaded and lucite bags, clothes, and sunglasses from the turn of the 20th century to the 1970s.

Luce House Antiques (18 Beach Rd., tel. 508/693–6440), in the landmark 1797 Luce House, specializes in Eastern European painted furniture and garden antiques. They will ship anywhere in the continental United States.

Menagerie (10 Union St., tel. 508/696–7650) is a great source of authentic vintage chenille and original clothes for children and women made from vintage fabrics.

In addition to its stock of interesting antiques, island crafts, jewelry, and handmade soaps and candles, **Pyewacket's** (135 Beach Rd., tel. 508/696–7766) provides a bit of magic—owner Karen Coffey reads tarot cards upstairs from the shop.

Art

Made Here (Main St. Courtyard, tel. 508/693–9429) boasts "Island art by island artists." Look for fanciful kinetic ceramic figures by Jenik Munafo and fun flower, fruit, and vegetable furniture by Hoke.

Shaw Cramer Gallery (76 Main St., 2nd floor, tel. 508/696–7323) carries one-of-a-kind and limited-edition crafts and paintings by nationally known artists and top island artists.

Books

Bunch of Grapes Bookstore (44 Main St., tel. 508/693–2291) carries a wide selection of fiction and nonfiction, including many island-related titles, and sponsors book signings—watch the papers for announcements.

Clothes

Alley Cat and Shoes by Arche (38 Main St., tel. 508/693–6970) is worth a stop just for its clever display windows. Inside there's great women's clothing in a cool, comfortable atmosphere.

Amelia Bloomers (30 Main St., tel. 508/693–9064) carries clothes for all occasions and a large array of cotton nightgowns and sleepwear—perfect for hot Vineyard nights.

Animals (4 Main St., tel. 508/696–4566) has cornered the market on cute, handmade children's clothes. The animal-theme togs come in sizes up to 10 and can be personalized.

Brickman's (8 Main St., tel. 508/693–0047) sells sportswear, surf-style clothing, and major-label footwear for the whole family. It also carries beach and sports gear, such as camping, fishing, and snorkeling equipment, and boogie boards and lots of toys and games for those occasional rainy days.

Hattitudes (Main St. Courtyard, tel. 508/696–8386) carries an enormous variety of hats from derbies and top hats to mile-wide straws and unusual bridal headpieces.

Hellie's Closet (3 Centre St., tel. 508/693–5828) is a consignment shop with great buys on previously owned designer and name-brand women's and children's clothes and shoes, many with their original tags. There are lots of retired wedding dresses, too.

Lorraine Parish (18 S. Main St., tel. 508/693–9044) designs and sells sophisticated, upscale women's dresses, suits, and blouses in natural fibers; and, just in case you forgot that dress you planned to wear for an island wedding, she carries lots of floaty chiffons. She also designed Carly Simon's wedding dress.

Murray's of the Vineyard (43 Main St., tel. 508/693–2640; Circuit Ave., Oak Bluffs, tel. 508/693–3743), a sister shop of Nantucket's Murray's Toggery, carries the ubiquitous, all-cotton Nantucket red pants, which fade to pink with washing.

Food

Cronig's Market (State Rd., tel. 508/693–4457) supports local farmers and specialty-item producers and offers a great selection of produce and other edibles.

Vineyard Gourmet (Main St., tel. 508/693–5181) stocks gourmet foods produced on-island and from around the world.

Home Accessories

All Things Oriental (123 Beach Rd., tel. 508/693–8375) has jewelry, porcelains, paintings, furniture, and more, all with an Asian theme.

The **Beach House** (off Main St., behind Paper Tiger, tel. 508/693–6091) stocks a large assortment of Italian pottery, linens, and party supplies. It's a great source for bridal and shower gifts.

Bowl and Board (35 Main St., tel. 508/693–9441) is summer-home central. It carries everything you need to cozy up a summer rental.

Bramhall & Dunn (19 Main St., tel. 508/693–6437) has fine crafts, linens, and housewares including outstanding quilts and innovative rag rugs by Judi Boisson. It also carries hand-knit sweaters and unique women's accessories and shoes.

Jewelry

The **Golden Basket** (52 Main St., tel. 508/696–7773; Kelley House, Dock and Kelly Sts., Edgartown, tel. 508/627-4459) specializes in jewelry versions of Nantucket lightship baskets.

Momilani Black Pearl (26 Main St., tel. 508/696–8828) features the Joryel Vera collection of black pearl and unique stones in affordable jewelry.

Moonstone (12 Main St., tel. 508/693–3367) offers estate jewelry and unique designs incorporating colorful and unusual stones. Artisans create many original pieces with nautical and island themes, and there is both a gemologist and jeweler on staff. Ask about the cuff links, tie tacks, pendants, and rings cast from the jacket button of the last civilian West Chop lighthouse keeper.

Sioux Eagle Designs (29 Main St., tel. 508/693–6537) sells unusual handmade jewelry from around the world. This is the place for quality wampum jewelry by Joan LeLacheur.

C. B. Stark Jewelers (53A Main St., tel. 508/693–2284; N. Water St., Edgartown, tel. 508/627–1260) creates one-of-a-kind pieces for both women and men, including island charms and custom work in 14- and 18-karat gold and platinum. It also carries other fine jewelry and watches. The Edgartown shop is smaller but has a more upscale inventory.

Odds and Ends

Black Dog General Store (between the Black Dog Tavern and the Bakery on Water St., tel. 508/696–8182) sells T-shirts, sweatshirts, beach towels, and many other gift items, all emblazoned with the telltale Black Dog. Merchandise is also available in the **Black Dog Cafe** (157 State Rd., tel. 508/696–8190), the **Black Dog Catalog Store** (162 State Rd., tel. 508/696–6059), and the **Black Dog General Store** in Edgartown (N. Summer St., tel. 508/627-3360).

Church Street (off Main St.) is a little enclave of shops including **Vineyard Sound Herbs** (tel. 508/696–7574) which sells skin-care products, soaps, and aromatherapy oils; **Fleece Dreams** (tel. 508/693–6141), which features handmade clothes in sumptuous fabrics; **Good Impressions** (tel. 508/693–7682), which sells rubber stamp supplies and has classes in stamp art and fabric embossing; and **Beadnicks** (tel. 508/693–7650), a bead lover's paradise.

Martha's Vineyard Women's Cooperative (Tisbury Marketplace, Beach Rd., tel. 508/693–2314) carries island-made crafts, including doll clothes that fit American Girl dolls. The Lydia Palmer jams and jellies sold here are terrific.

Midnight Farm (18 Water-Cromwell La., tel. 508/693–1997) is co-owned by Carly Simon and Tamara Weiss and stocks funky furniture, clothes, shoes, jewelry, linens, dinnerware, books, soaps, candles, garden supplies, snack foods, and, of course, Carly's books and CDs.

Nothing extends the feeling of vacation like viewing your snapshots on the way home. **Mosher Photo** (25 Main St., tel. 508/693–9430) carries a full line of cameras—both disposable and non—and can process your pictures within three hours. Best of all, it's close to the ferry.

Paper Tiger (29 Main St., tel. 508/693–8970) offers a wide array of handmade paper, cards, and gift items, plus wind chimes, pottery, writing utensils, and works by local artists. Check out the mini-mobiles over the counter.

Wind's Up! (199 Beach Rd., tel. 508/693–4340) sells swimwear, windsurfing and sailing equipment, boogie boards, and other outdoor gear.

OAK BLUFFS
Antiques

Argonauta of Martha's Vineyard (73 Circuit Ave., tel. 508/696–0097) offers antique furniture and reproductions made from antique materials at very reasonable prices. It'll ship anywhere in the continental United States.

In a Campgrounds cottage, tucked behind Circuit Avenue, **Never Say Goodbye** (55 Samoset Ave., tel. 508/693–9313) sports an extensive collection of vintage linens, clothes, and jewelry displayed on the porch and lawn. Inside, there's more, including a whole rack of satiny antique kimonos.

Oak Bluffs Flea Market (8 Uncas Ave. [off Upper Circuit Ave.], tel. 508/696–0700) is a conglomeration of more than 25 antiques dealers under one roof. You'll find furniture, architectural salvage, vintage clothing and jewelry, classic fishing gear, and lots of nautical and island memorabilia. The market also offers coffee, cold drinks, and baked goods as a nice break from shopping. There's lots of free parking.

Tuckernuck Antiques (79 Tuckernuck [off Upper Circuit Ave.], tel. 508/696–6392) carries oak Victorian and early American pine furniture, as well as an extensive collection of old island postcards and other memorabilia.

Art

Cousen Rose Gallery (71 Circuit Ave., tel. 508/693–6656) has works by many island artists including Myrna Morris, John Breckenridge, Marietta Cleasby, Deborah Colter, and Will Savage. Don't miss Janice Frame's "Dolls of the Gullah Region." They are sumptuous. And, to keep junior artists happy, there's paper and crayons on a table right inside the door.

Dragonfly Gallery (Dukes County and Vineyard Aves., tel. 508/ 693–8877) changes shows weekly and holds artist receptions every other Saturday during the summer from 4 to 7 PM, featuring amazing jazz pianist John Alaimo. Check the local papers for a schedule of artists.

The **Firehouse Gallery** (635 Dukes County Ave., at Vineyard Ave., tel. 508/693–9025) is home to the Martha's Vineyard Center for the Visual Arts. It holds weekly shows throughout the summer, featuring island and off-island artists. Check the local paper for receptions and featured artists.

Books

Book Den East (New York Ave., tel. 508/693–3946) is an amazing place to browse and buy, with 20,000 out-of-print, antiquarian, and paperback books housed in an old barn.

Clothes

Island Outfitters (Post Office Sq. [off Circuit Ave.], tel. 508/693–5003) will blind you with its extensive line of tropical prints by Lilly Pulitzer, Tommy Bahama, Jams World, and more.

The gorgeous dresses hanging in the window of **Laughing Bear** (33 Circuit Ave., tel. 508/693–9342) will lure you into the store. Inside you'll find women's wear made of Balinese or Indian batiks and other unusual materials, plus jewelry and accessories from around the world. Although the goods are pricey, there's a great sale rack.

Slight Indulgence (Post Office Sq., tel. 508/693–8194) is best known for its sterling jewelry from all over the world; but the long, floaty, layered batik and African print dresses are not to be missed.

Odds and Ends

If you're looking for out-of-the-ordinary, **Craftworks** (42 Circuit Ave., tel. 508/693–7463) carries outrageous painted furniture, ceramic figures, and home accessories—all handmade by American artists.

Good Dog Goods (79 Circuit Ave., tel. 508/696–7100) is doggie heaven. You'll find all-natural dog foods and homemade biscuits, as well as dog-related items for humans. The back room is the "Bakery," where an old-fashioned display case houses healthy doggie pastries that look so enticing they'll make your own mouth water. Four-legged shoppers are welcome.

The **Secret Garden** (41 Circuit Ave., tel. 508/693–4759), set in a yellow gingerbread cottage, has a complete line of Shelia collectibles—miniature wooden versions of Camp Ground houses and other island landmarks.

Sky's the Limit (39 Circuit Ave., tel. 508/693–8261) lives up to its name with a store covered with kites. There's a wide selection of other toys and games, too.

EDGARTOWN
Antiques

Clocktower Antiques and Interiors (Nevin Square on Winter St., tel. 508/627–8006) is delightfully cluttered with antique silver, china, glassware, linens, toys, and more.

Vivian Wolfe Antiques (Winter St., tel. 508/627–5822) offers fine antique and estate jewelry, as well as antique silver tea services and the like.

Art

Edgartown Scrimshaw Gallery (17 N. Water St., tel. 508/627–9439) showcases a large collection of scrimshaw, including some antique pieces, as well as Nantucket lightship baskets and 14-karat lightship-basket jewelry.

The **Old Sculpin Gallery** (58 Dock St. [next to the Chappy Ferry], tel. 508/627–4881) is the Martha's Vineyard Art Association's headquarters. Only original art by island artists is on display in this building, which dates back before 1800. Don't miss the fabulous seaweed collages by Rose Treat.

Willoughby's (12 N. Water St., tel. 508/627–3369) displays mostly island landscapes and scenes by Vineyard and Cape artists, including limited-edition prints and drawings.

Books

Dana Anderson and Marilyn Scheerbaum, co-owners of **Bickerton & Ripley Books** (Main and S. Summer Sts., tel. 508/627–8463), are true bibliophiles. They carry a large selection of current and island-related titles and will be happy to make a recommendation for your easy summer reading.

Clothes

Brickman's (33 Main St., tel. 508/697–4700) sells sportswear, surf-style clothing, and major-label footwear for the family.

The Casual Code: How to Look Like a Local

There's a saying among islanders: if you step off the ferry in a suit, you're either marrying someone or burying someone. The moral? Dress up and you'll be instantly pegged as an outsider. There's a practical side to the island's casual dress code—city clothes just don't work on the island. High-heeled shoes that are perfectly fine on city sidewalks will sink in the sand, aerate lawns, and impede your progress up Circuit Avenue on Saturday night. Wear chinos, sandals, T-shirts, or wrinkled linen and you'll fit right in. Black Dog gear and Nantucket red pants are very popular on the mainland, but wear them on the Vineyard and you'll instantly stick out as someone who just got off the boat (or plane).

What do the locals wear? Wampum, beads that are made from shells and fashioned into jewelry—especially bracelets. Although expensive (well-made ones start at around $500), there are island women who will wear multiple wampum bracelets circling their wrists, sometimes alternated with sea glass jewelry. If you need directions, look for a man or woman wearing a wampum bracelet. Chances are excellent that he or she knows the lay of the land.

Chica (12A N. Water St., tel. 508/627–9661) carries hip, funky, and ethnic clothes for young skinny women and loose linens for the rest of us.

Dream Weaver (1 S. Water St., tel. 508/627–9683) purports to be "a gallery of art to wear," and that's pretty accurate. It features clothing and accessories produced by the top 100 fiber artists in the world, and the stock is absolutely dazzling. Everything is handmade of the most luxurious fabrics, furs, and yarns. Prices are very steep, but if you're looking for something special to wear, bite the bullet and indulge. There's usually a sale rack upstairs.

Forgot to pack that gown or tuxedo? **Sentimental Journey** (261 Upper Main St., tel. 508/627–7597) carries special-occasion and bridal wear at reasonable prices. The shop stocks lots of Jessica and Scott McClintock and other great designers. It also does emergency tuxedo rentals and sales.

Sweaters, Inc. (5 Winter St., tel. 508/627–9207) showcases mostly handmade sweaters, tops, coats, and jackets for women from surprisingly inexpensive to over the top. Look for the marvelously colored sweaters by Dia.

Whistling Fish (Dock St., tel. 508/627–7368) features children's clothing in sizes 0 to 14. There are many great labels including Lilly Pulitzer, Blue Ginger, and Monkey Monkey.

Jewelry

Optional Art (35 Winter St., tel. 508/627–5373) carries fine jewelry in 18-karat gold and platinum, handcrafted by more than 25 top American artisans. You'll pay a lot, but the inventory here isn't typical of other island shops.

Claudia (35 Winter St., tel. 508/627–8306; 34 Main St., Vineyard Haven, tel. 508/693–5465) brings you back to another era with its clever windows, antique display cases, and fabulous French fragrances. You'll find designer, vintage-looking, and fine gold and silver jewelry in a variety of price ranges. The Vineyard Haven location is a slightly smaller shop.

Odds and Ends

Fligors (27 N. Water St., tel. 508/627–4722) is the closest thing to a department store on the island. A large room upstairs houses an extensive and beautifully displayed line of ceramic Christmas village items by manufacturer Dept. 56. The rest of the store is filled with children's clothing, Vineyard-theme books and ties, Byers' Christmas Carolers, and lots more.

In the Woods (55 Main St., tel. 508/627–8989) is a large store that features nearly every type of wood in almost any guise. Try out the comfy Adirondack chairs out front while you view the clever birch-bark birdhouses in the window. It's a great source for wooden salad bowls.

Once in a Blue Moon (22 Winter St., tel. 508/627–9177) carries high-quality contemporary ceramics, textiles, turned wood, lamps and mirrors, small paintings, and furniture. The hand-painted silk wall hangings by Kathy Schorr are worth the visit.

For those who like to keep busy, even on vacation, **Vineyard Stitches** (9 Winter St., tel. 508/627–8212) is the perfect place to pick up an island-theme needlepoint kit. It stocks distinctive hand-painted canvases and other needlepoint supplies. Look for island lighthouse kits in a basket near the door.

UP-ISLAND

WEST TISBURY
Antiques

Hull Antiques (Edgartown Rd. [look for sign and a ladderback chair hanging on a tree], tel. 508/693–5713) specializes in decoys, sterling, folk art, and Early American furniture. What you won't find here are reproductions and fussy gifts.

Legal Antiques (496 State Rd., tel. 508/696–7820) showcases reasonably priced antique furniture. The vintage quilts are in good shape and moderately priced.

Art

Chilmark Pottery (Fieldview La., off State Rd., tel. 508/693–6476) is a workshop and gallery selling hand-formed stoneware, porcelain, and Raku-ware mostly by island potters.

Craven Gallery (459 State Rd., tel. 508/693–3535) showcases contemporary paintings, drawings, photography, and ceramics.

The **Field Gallery and Sculpture Garden** (State Rd., tel. 508/693–5595) is a good source for works by local artists. Tom Maley's whimsical sculptures grace the garden, and Heather Goff's tile murals are a treat.

The **Granary Gallery** (Red Barn Emporium, Old County Rd., tel. 508/693–0455) exhibits artworks by island and international artists and displays Early American furniture. Don't miss the back room, where black-and-white photos by Margaret Bourke White, Norman Bergsma, Arthur Rickerby, and Alfred Eisenstaedt line the walls. Prices begin at around $350 for a small acrylic to approximately $50,000 for a limited-edition print of Eisenstaedt's famous "V.J. Day Kiss" photo.

To find **Hermine Merel Smith Fine Art** (Edgartown Rd., tel. 508/693–7719) watch for the sign and the mounds of impatiens at the entrance. Then step through the beautiful, arched glass doors to the cool, quiet interior, where fine paintings and works on paper by Vineyard and national artists are on display.

At **Martha's Vineyard Glassworks** (State Rd., tel. 508/693–6026) you can pick out a beautiful art-glass gift and then watch the glass blowers at their craft. The service here is friendly and the staff is knowledgeable.

Vineyard Arts and Crafts Fairs (Grange Hall, State Rd., tel. 508/693–8989) bring shoppers into direct contact with Vineyard artists and artisans. They're held from 10 to 2 on Sundays in June and September and Sundays and Thursdays in July and August. Look for the whimsical art furniture of Ted Box, island seascapes by Millie Briggs, and limited-edition toned gelatin prints by Janet Woodcock.

Vineyard Artisans Festivals(tel. 508/693–8989) are special shows held at either the Grange Hall (State Road) or the Agricultural Hall (35 Panhandle Road). They include the Vineyard Artisans Labor Day Festival, Holiday Festival, and the Vineyard Furniture Show. Check the local papers or call the phone number listed above for times, dates, and locations.

Food

Cronig's Market (489 State Rd., tel. 508/693–2234) is a smaller version of the Down-Island store.

West Tisbury Farmers' Market—with booths selling fresh flowers, plants, fruits and vegetables, honey, and homemade baked goods and jams—is held at the Grange Hall (State Rd., tel. 508/693–9549) mid-June to mid-October, Saturdays from 9 to noon and Wednesdays from 2:30 to 5:30.

Odds and Ends

Alley's General Store (State Rd., tel. 508/693–0088), in business since 1858, deals in everything from fresh fruit and preserves to shoelaces, suntan lotions, and video rentals. There's even a post office.

North Tisbury (State Rd., West Tisbury) is a small shopping district that includes **Craven Gallery** (tel. 508/693–3535), a little shop that carries original artwork by local and nationally known artists; **Conroy Apothecary** (tel. 508/693–7070), with its harried but cheerful pharmacists and shelves full of suntan lotions, greeting cards, and other necessities; and **Biga Bakery & Deli** (tel. 508/693–6924), a great place to pick up fresh bread, gooey pastries, or a deli sandwich.

CHILMARK

The shop at **Allen Farm** (South Rd., tel. 508/645–9064) has handwoven blankets and knitted items made from the farm's wool. Prices range from $165 for a simple sweater to $600 for something a bit more complicated.

Chilmark Chocolates (State Rd., tel. 508/645–3013) sells superior chocolates and the world's finest butter crunch, which you can sometimes watch being made in the back room. It also employs a large percentage of the island's handicapped. Don't forget to pick up a catalog—mail orders are available except during warm months.

MENEMSHA

On your way to watching the sun set at the beach on Menemsha Bight, visit the clothing and crafts shops that line **Basin Road.**

Don't expect much in the way of bargains at the Menemsha shops, however, as these stores are strictly seasonal.

Right at the Bight (tel. 508/645–3747) carries quality women's wear from beach to business to formal; **Pandora's Box** (tel. 508/645–9696) stocks unique, expensive, quality fashions for women, as well as soaps and gifts; **Vineyard Blues** (tel. 508/645–3800) sells casual clothes for men, women, and children, most adorned with the shop's trademark embroidered bluefish. **Jane N. Slater** (tel. 508/645–3348) stocks Fiestaware, depression-era glass, and antique silver, china, and furniture. **Up on the Roof** (tel. 508/645–3735) gets its name from the friendly dog that hangs out on the roof of the shop, which is home to lots of tacky, silly signs and sayings in faux antique and primitive frames. **Harbor Craft Shop** (tel. 508/645–2929 or 508/645–2655) carries a not particularly distinctive line of gifts, soaps, and home goods, but it's nicely fragrant inside.

AQUINNAH

A small group of souvenir and crafts shops cater to the day-trippers who load off the buses at Aquinnah Circle for a view of the Aquinnah Cliffs. You'll have no trouble finding the T-shirt or refrigerator magnet of your dreams in one of the several visitor-oriented shops, but you can also find Native American (specifically Wampanoag) crafts. Most notable for their wares are the **Aquinnah Shop** (tel. 508/645–3142), where Wampanoag medicine man Luther Madison mans the two small counters that include the excellent wampum jewelry of tribe member Donald Widdiss, and **Stony Creek Gifts** (tel. 508/645–3595), which carries hand-made Native American crafts, including wampum and dream catchers, mostly from the Southwest.

Beyond T-Shirts and Key Chains

You can't go wrong with baseball caps, refrigerator magnets, beer mugs, sweatshirts, T-shirts, key chains, and other local logo merchandise. You won't go broke buying these items, either.

BUDGET FOR A MAJOR PURCHASE If souvenirs are all about keeping the memories alive in the long haul, plan ahead to shop for something really special—a work of art, a rug or something else hand-crafted, or a major accessory for your home. One major purchase will stay with you far longer than a dozen tourist trinkets, and you'll have all the wonderful memories associated with shopping for it besides.

ADD TO YOUR COLLECTION Whether antiques, used books, salt and pepper shakers, or ceramic frogs are your thing, start looking in the first day or two. Chances are you'll want to scout around and then go back to some of the first shops you visited before you hand over your credit card.

GET GUARANTEES IN WRITING Is the vendor making promises? Ask him to put them in writing.

ANTICIPATE A SHOPPING SPREE If you think you might buy breakables, include a length of bubble wrap. Pack a large tote bag in your suitcase in case you need extra space. Don't fill your suitcase to bursting before you leave home. Or include some old clothing that you can leave behind to make room for new acquisitions.

KNOW BEFORE YOU GO Study prices at home on items you might consider buying while you're away. Otherwise you won't recognize a bargain when you see one.

PLASTIC, PLEASE Especially if your purchase is pricey and you're looking for authenticity, it's always smart to pay with a credit card. If a problem arises later on and the merchant can't or won't resolve it, the credit-card company may help you out.

If you're not a beach person, you may be in the wrong place. If you do love beaches, point your nose in any direction and proceed to romantic fulfillment. The reputation of the Vineyard's varied beaches is well deserved. They rank among the world's top surf-and-sand destinations. And even if you don't have access to every strip of sand, there are plenty of swatches tucked away in hidden corners that will bring out the Robinson Crusoe in you.

In This Chapter

By Perry Garfinkel

beaches

YOU COME TO AN ISLAND FOR ITS BEACHES. On Martha's Vineyard, you will not be disappointed. Although just 75 mi in circumference, the island has enough varieties of the elemental meeting of land and water to fulfill the fantasies of every Gilligan. Quiet coves, beaches along freshwater ponds, big waves splashing up against soft white sand, gentle ones lapping up to a shoreline, tidal pools, rocky coastlines, dramatic cliffs falling into the ocean, clay pits—they're all here. Some beaches are open to anyone with an appetite for wet: that is, they are open to the public. Others are owned by the towns they're in and require a pass or sticker, which you can buy from the individual towns' parks and recreation departments (in the town halls). Still others are privately owned by individuals or beach clubs (such as the East Chop Beach Club in Oak Bluffs, Quansoo in Chilmark, and Seven Gates in West Tisbury), requiring you to know people in high places with access to these private paradises. And there is another category: the off-the-beaten-track beach that requires an adventurous spirit, the willingness to walk a bit, and good directions. These are open to the public.

As you will read, many are overseen by island land conservation organizations, such as the Land Bank, the Sheriff's Meadow Foundation, and the Trustees of Reservation. All adhere to the time-honored environmentalist's credo: take only pictures, leave only footprints.

The north shore of the island faces Vineyard Sound. The beaches on this side have more gentle waters; they're also often slightly less chilly. On a clear day you can see across the sound to the chain of Elizabeth Islands, Cape Cod, and sometimes even all the way to New Bedford, Massachusetts.

The south shore—18 mi from the Aquinnah Cliffs east to South Beach in Katama, said to be among the longest continuous uninterrupted stretches of white-sand beach from Georgia to Maine—faces the Atlantic Ocean. Not only is it an endless beach, there's not a single condo complex, high-rise hotel, or apartment building along the shore. On the Vineyard's south shore, surf from the Atlantic Ocean crashes up to the shore in refreshingly chilly waves—a great place for body- or board-surfing or for just letting the ebb and flow of the tides mesmerize you.

Note that some public beaches, such as the Joseph A. Sylvia State Beach and South Beach in Edgartown, have free parking along the road or in a lot. Others, such as Moshup Beach in Aquinnah, charge a fee for parking in a lot.

DOWN-ISLAND

VINEYARD HAVEN (TISBURY)

Lake Tashmoo Town Beach (end of Herring Creek Rd.) invites swimming in the warm, relatively shallow, brackish lake or in the cooler, gentle Vineyard Sound. There is a lifeguarded area and some parking.

Owen Park Beach (off Main S.), a small, sandy harbor beach, has a children's play area, lifeguards, and a harbor view. The beach straddles a dock that juts into the harbor and is just steps away from the ferry terminal in Vineyard Haven, making it a great spot for some last rays and a dip before you have to kiss the island good-bye.

Tisbury Town Beach (end of Owen Little Way off Main St.) is a public beach next to the Vineyard Haven Yacht Club. As at Owen

Park Beach, its proximity to the town makes it a perfect out-of-the-way yet near-everything spot for a quick escape from the crowds and a dip.

OAK BLUFFS

Eastville Beach (just over the bridge on Beach Rd. leading from Vineyard Haven to Oak Bluffs) is a small beach where children enjoy swimming in the calm waters and diving off the pilings under the draw bridge. From the shore you can watch boats of all sizes passing under the bridge between the lagoon and the harbor.

Joseph A. Sylvia State Beach (between Oak Bluffs and Edgartown off Beach Rd.) is a 6-mi-long sandy beach with a view of Cape Cod across Nantucket Sound. The calm, warm water and food vendors make it popular with families. There's parking along the roadside, and the beach is accessible by bike path or shuttle bus. Across the street from this barrier beach is Sengekontacket Pond, a popular fishing and shellfishing spot. Even if you don't love beaches, the drive and the expansive vista of the sound and the pond alone will make you at least develop a severe case of infatuation.

Oak Bluffs Town Beach (between the steamship dock and the state beach off Sea View Ave.) is a crowded, narrow stretch of calm water on Nantucket Sound, with snack stands, lifeguards, roadside parking, and rest rooms at the steamship office. One section has been nicknamed Inkwell Beach by the generations of African Americans who summer on the Vineyard and have been enjoying this stretch for more than a century. There's a changing area and showers in this section as well.

EDGARTOWN

Bend-in-the-Road Beach (Beach Rd.), Edgartown's town beach, is a protected area marked by floats adjacent to Joseph A. Sylvia State Beach. Backed by low, grassy dunes and wild roses, Bend-

Dune Diligence

Every beach you visit will have signs asking—as politely as they can—that you keep off the dunes. That is not because islanders want to keep the place looking like Martha Stewart's backyard. The dunes play an integral part in maintaining the delicate ecological balance that makes this island so appealing—and such a unique environmental gem. Mounds of sand, the dunes play an important role in storm damage prevention and flood control. They provide buffer from storm waves for landward properties and coastal wetlands. They are also the homes and source of food for the wildlife here, birds such as terns and gulls who nest at their bases. In addition, the plants that grow among the dunes plenish the ocean water with nutrients that eventually break down and become a food source for fish and other marine life.

So, though inviting they may be to stroll through and cooler their sand may be for burning feet, if you are hoping to return to the island next year and see it just the way you saw it this season, respect the wishes of the environmental groups and parks and recreation officials who post the signs.

in-the-Road has calm, shallow waters; some parking; and lifeguards. It is on the shuttle bus and bike routes.

Little Beach (end of Fuller St.) is a little-known beach that looks like a crooked pinkie that points into Eel Pond, a great place for bird-watching (be careful of the fenced-off Piping Plover breeding grounds in the dunes). From here you can look across and see the lighthouse at Cape Poge, at the northern tip of Chappaquiddick. This is a great beach for quiet sunbathing and shallow water wading. There's limited streetside parking along Fuller Street. From Pease Point Way, turn right onto Morse Street, then left to Fuller.

Lighthouse Beach is accessible from North Water Street or by continuing toward downtown Edgartown from Little Beach. The beach wraps around the Edgartown Lighthouse, a classic backdrop for wedding pictures. Though you will have no privacy, as many strollers pass along here, it commands a great view of all of Edgartown Harbor.

South Beach (Katama Rd.), also called Katama Beach, is the island's largest and most popular. A 3-mi ribbon of sand on the Atlantic, it sustains strong surf and occasional dangerous riptides, so check with the lifeguards before swimming. Also check the weather conditions, as fog can quickly turn a glorious blue-sky morning here into what seems like an afternoon in London. There is limited parking.

CHAPPAQUIDDICK ISLAND

East Beach, one of the area's best beaches, is accessible by car from Chappaquiddick Road to Dyke Road, or by boat or Jeep from the Wasque Reservation (☞ Chapter 4). It has heavy surf, good bird-watching, and relative isolation in a lovely setting. There is a $3 fee to enter the beach.

Wasque Beach, at the Wasque Reservation (☞ Chapter 4), is an uncrowded ½-mi sandy beach with sometimes strong surf and currents, a parking lot, and rest rooms.

UP-ISLAND

WEST TISBURY

To reach **Cedar Tree Neck Wildlife Sanctuary,** take Indian Hill Road to Obed Dagget Road, a dirt road that leads to the trailhead of this Sheriff's Meadow Foundation conservation area. From the ample parking area, the trailhead leads through an enchanted forest down a hill, across a tiny foot bridge, and over dunes to a long beach with giant boulders. This is not a swimming beach, but it invites long, contemplative walks.

To Beach His Own

There's good news and bad news, depending on your bent. Vineyard beaches are not like others in popular resort destinations. You won't find hot dog and ice cream stands; nor will you find vendors walking up and down the beaches trying to sell you local trinkets. You won't see hotels and condos lining any of the beaches. There are no lounges or umbrella stands, or people selling or renting either. You will not find man-made or, for that matter, nature-made protection from the sun. However, if a pristine beach experience is what you're looking for, you've come to the right place.

In light of this, adopt the motto: be prepared. If you need creature comforts, you'll have to bring them yourself. Along with the usual suggestion to pack plenty of sunscreen, wear a hat, and bring beach towels, it's highly advisable to pack water and juice and something to eat, as you will not find such items for sale once you're at the beach. Once you've toted your haul to the sand, lie back and enjoy—you're in calm, clutter-free surroundings.

Lambert's Cove Beach (Lambert's Cove Rd.), one of the island's prettiest, has fine sand and very clear water. The Vineyard Sound–side beach has calm waters good for children and views of the Elizabeth Islands. In season it is restricted to residents and those staying in West Tisbury.

Long Point Wildlife Refuge, a Trustees of Reservations preserve, has a beautiful beach on the Atlantic, as well as freshwater and saltwater ponds for swimming, including the brackish Tisbury Great Pond. There are rest rooms.

Sepiessa Point Reservation (off Tiah's Cove Rd.) is a 164-acre area of the Land Bank Commission. There's parking for only a few cars at the trailhead, so consider yourself warned. A long walk along Tiah's Cove leads to a beach, at the southerly point, alongside Tisbury Great Pond. Across the pond you can see the ocean. The very narrow beach is delightful, though not for laying out a towel and sunbathing. Those with canoes or kayaks can put in at the trailhead and paddle across the pond to a barrier beach for picnicking and swimming.

Uncle Seth's Pond is a warm freshwater pond on Lambert's Cove Road, with a small beach right off the road. Seth's is very popular with families—toddlers enjoy frolicking in the shallow waters along the shore—as well as with the lap swimmers criss-crossing the pond. Car parking is very limited.

CHILMARK

Chilmark Pond Preserve (off South Rd.), on the south side of the road about 3 mi from West Tisbury Center, is an 8-acre Land Bank property at the foot of Abel's Hill (look for the white post with the Land Bank signage). From a landing at the bottom of the driveway, you reach the north side of magnificent Chilmark Lower Pond. You can either plant yourself right there or, if you bring your own canoe, kayak, small row boat, or inflatable raft, you can paddle a very short distance across the pond to 200 ft of Land Bank–owned Atlantic Ocean beach. If you're not a Chilmark resident or Chilmark summer renter with a beach pass, this is the only public Atlantic Ocean beach access in town. There is parking for about 10 cars.

Lucy Vincent Beach (off South Rd.), on the south shore, is one of the island's most beautiful. The wide strand of fine sand is backed by high clay bluffs facing the Atlantic surf. Keep walking to the left (east, or Down-Island) to reach the unofficial nude beach. Walking to the right, toward the private Windy Gates beach, is restricted to those who own beachfront property here. All others are prohibited. There's great bodysurfing for all ages in these waters. In season, Lucy Vincent is restricted to town residents and visitors with passes. Off-season a stroll here is the perfect getaway. Parking is available.

A narrow beach that is part smooth rocks and pebbles, part fine sand, **Squibnocket Beach** (off South Rd.), on the south shore, offers an appealing boulder-strewn coastline and gentle waves. Surfers know this area for its good waves. Tide-pool lovers will appreciate the opportunity to study marine life close up. During the season, this beach is restricted to residents and visitors with passes.

MENEMSHA

Great Rock Bight Preserve (on North Rd., about 1 mi from the Menemsha Hills Reservation) is a Land Bank–managed tract of 28 acres. Parking is at the end of a ½-mi dirt road; it's a ½-mi walk to the beach, a secluded sandy cove of about 1,300 ft. It's well worth the trek.

Menemsha Beach (adjacent to Dutcher's Dock) is a pebbly public beach with gentle surf on Vineyard Sound and, with views to the northwest, a great place to catch the sunset. This is an active harbor for both commercial and sport fishermen; you'll be able to catch an eyeful of the handsome yachts and smaller boats. There are always anglers working the tides on the jetty, too. On site are rest rooms and lifeguards. Snack stands and restaurants are a short walk from the parking lot, which can get crowded in summer (there's room for about 60 cars).

Menemsha Hills Reservation (off North Rd., on the left about 1 mi Down-Island coming from the Menemsha Cross Road) is administered by the Trustees of Reservation. From the parking lot, it's 1 mi to the second-highest point on the island, Prospect Hill (308 ft), with a spectacular view. Then it's another mile on the Upper Trail to Great Sand Cliffs and the rocky shoreline of Vineyard Sound.

AQUINNAH

Lobsterville Beach encompasses 2 mi of beautiful sand and dune beach directly off Lobsterville Road on the Vineyard Sound. It's a seagull nesting area and a favorite fishing spot. Though the water tends to be cold, and the pebbles along the shore make getting in and out difficult, the beach is protected and suitable for children. The view looking east—of Menemsha Harbor, the rest of the Vineyard, and the Elizabeth Islands across the sound—makes you feel like you're surrounded by the Greek islands. There is limited public parking for about eight cars. Given the limited parking, this is an ideal stop-off for cyclists exploring this area of the island.

Moshup Beach (at intersection of State Rd. and Moshup Trail) is, according to the Land Bank, "probably the most glamorous" of its holdings, because the beach provides access to the awesome Aquinnah Cliffs. The best views of the cliffs and up to the lighthouse are from a 25-plus-minute walk via boardwalk and beach. On clear days Nomans Land looms like a giant mirage. There is a drop-off area close to the beach, but you still must park in the lot and walk to the sand. The island shuttle bus stops here, too, and there are bike racks on the beach. Come early in the day to ensure both a quieter experience and an available parking spot. Keep in mind that climbing the cliffs is against the law—they're eroding much too quickly on their own. It's also illegal to take any of the clay with you. There's a parking fee of $15 from Memorial Day to Labor Day.

Philbin Beach, off Moshup Trail, is restricted to town residents or renters with a lease. It's a nice wide beach with a wild Atlantic Ocean challenging you to master it. Beach passes can be obtained from the Aquinnah town hall (65 State Rd., tel. 508/ 645–2300).

You brought the tennis racket. You brought the kayak. You brought the fishing gear. You brought the bikes, the roller blades, the inflatable raft, the volleyball and net, the hiking boots, the golf clubs—in fact, you expended so much energy schlepping all this gear that now you're too tired to do anything. Beach, anyone?

In This Chapter

By Perry Garfinkel

outdoor activities and sports

SOME VISITORS COME TO MARTHA'S VINEYARD for the sheer pleasure of letting their eyes rest on some of the most soothing sights nature has ever painted. Others come to rub elbows with celebrities or to imagine themselves one. Still others come to paint or write—or simply think quiet thoughts. Some come just to put a body of water between their daily concerns and the way they would much rather live. But the smart ones come to be outdoors and active. They come to fish—or to act like one. They come to play tennis and golf, to hike and bike, to surf and sail—or whatever other excuse they can come up with to be outside.

The Vineyard is a playground. Some have described it as summer camp for adults. And while it's true that you can have a perfectly wonderful vacation shuttling back and forth to the beach every day—with breaks, of course, for fresh fish dinners; to really appreciate this island you have to dive into it head first. So put your mind to rest—bury your nose in some long postponed summer reading if you must give your mind some exercise—and put your body to the work of play. Body and mind will thank you.

BIKING

The down side first: you'll be sharing some winding roads with wide trucks and tour buses cruising right by your elbow, inexperienced moped riders, and automobile drivers unfamiliar with the island roads, not to mention other cyclists of various levels of experience. In addition, the roads are winding and most are bordered by sand—even those not near the beaches. The bottom line is this: pay attention at all times. And if ever there was a place to commit to wearing a helmet, this would be that place.

That said, the Vineyard is also a cyclist's paradise, and you don't have to be an experienced rider to enjoy the paths and roads here. With the highest elevation about 300 ft above sea level, this is relatively easy uphill and downhill biking with well-paved bike paths both Down-Island and Up. There are a couple of fun roller-coaster-like dips on the state-forest bike path. Watch out for the occasional inline skater on these paths. Quiet country roads wind up and down gentle hills covered by low-hanging trees that make you feel as though you're riding through a lush green tunnel. The views—across open fields to the Atlantic Ocean, alongside ponds with floating swans, or of sun-flecked meadows where handsome horses graze—will nearly knock you off your bike seat. There is another benefit: you'll be helping environmentalists who would rather see more non-polluting bikes here than carbon monoxide–spewing, fossil fuel–guzzling vehicles.

Maps of the island's paved bike paths are available at all rental shops and many other island shops. One of the best all-around maps, which includes bike trails, is the "Martha's Vineyard Detailed Road Map," published by Edward Thomas (Box 1354, Vineyard Haven 02568, tel. 508/693–2059).

Two of the quietest and most scenic roads without paths are North Road, from North Tisbury center all the way to Menemsha; and Middle Road, from its start at Music Street west to Beetlebung Corner, where South Road and Menemsha Cross Road intersect. The ride from there Up-Island to the western tip of the island in Aquinnah is challenging—winding and sandy roads with a steep hill or two—but worth the rewards of spectacular views.

For a shortcut to Aquinnah, take the bike ferry at the very end of North Road in Menemsha. The two-minute ride across the channel entering Menemsha Pond costs $4 one-way for bike and rider, $7 round-trip. There's no schedule; it makes the crossing when there are passengers.

Bringing your own bike would be the first choice, as you want a familiar and trusty steed below you (you will want to have the bike gears cleaned and checked before and after your sandy Vineyard biking experience). The round-trip fare for a bicycle on the ferry is $6 (in addition to the passenger fare of $10 round-trip). But there are also several bike rental shops here (listed below by town); bear in mind the only one up-island is in West Tisbury's town center.

CONSERVATION AREAS

Several island organizations are seeing to it that, no matter how many new houses are built here, there will always be open space protected from development. Not only are many of them acquiring and overseeing priceless chunks of Vineyard property, they're also educating year-round residents and seasonal visitors alike about the complex ecology of the island—and why it's so important to respect it.

The first request these groups usually make of visitors is to leave the environment they way they found it. Throwing cigarette butts out windows, leaving trash on beaches or aluminum cans and glass bottles wherever you please, trampling or picking plants and flowers—these are obvious no-nos. Even if you're here for a day trip, you can make a difference.

Conservation lands include beaches and woods that are accessible to the public and some that are not. The Martha's Vineyard Land Bank Commission, which acquires lands with revenue generated by a 2% public surcharge on most real estate transactions occurring in the six island towns, publishes a detailed map including the 42 Land Bank properties and descriptions, along with other conservation lands through the island. (Free copies may be obtained by writing Martha's

Vineyard Land Bank Commission, Box 2057, Edgartown, MA
02539.) Guided nature and bird-watching walks and self-tours
take place at many of these sites (☞ Hiking and Walking, *below*).

FISHING

Huge trawlers unload abundant daily catches at the docks in
Vineyard Haven and Menemsha, attesting to the richness of the
waters surrounding the island. Commercial fishing is an
important industry here, but some of the most zealous fishing is
done by amateurs. One of the most popular spots for sport
anglers is Wasque Point on Chappaquiddick. Two others are
South Beach and the jetty at the mouth of the Menemsha Basin.
But true to their salty character, savvy island fishers never reveal
where the fish are really "biting" on a given day. Striped bass
and bluefish are star island fish. The annual Striped Bass &
Bluefish Derby attracts fishing fanatics from all over the world
each fall. Several outfits offer deep-sea fishing trips if surf
fishing is not your thing. Individual fishing licenses are not
required.

If you know nothing about boats and fishing and want to get your
feet wet, so to speak, call Wendy Swolinzky at Book-A-Boat (tel.
508/645–2400). She'll connect you with fishing boats, sailboats,
and charters of all sorts. There is no charge for her service.

HIKING

The island's beaches get a lot of press—and deservedly so. Much
less heralded are the island's extensive walking and hiking trails,
overseen by various conservation groups. The nature preserves
and conservation areas are laced with well-marked, scenic trails
through varied terrains and ecological habitats. At the trailheads
of most are small parking areas and bulletin boards with maps
and other posted instructions, restrictions, directions, and
information. Note that some prohibit dogs; some allow them on
a leash.

Especially in summer, but throughout the fall and winter too, many island groups sponsor informative guided walks led by naturalists and other experts. Check the local weekly papers for schedules. For kids, Felix Neck Wildlife Sanctuary offers an extensive schedule of educational yet entertaining programs aimed at children—and adults too.

A word of warning: beware of poison ivy, recognized by its clusters of three shiny green leafs. In fall the leaves turn bright red and its white berries may be mistaken for bayberry fruit. Also, keep in mind that Martha's Vineyard's grassy brushy areas are popular hangouts for two types of ticks: wood ticks, which may carry Tularemia and Rocky Mountain Spotted Fever; and deer ticks, which may carry Babesiosis and Lyme Disease. For more information, drop by the **Martha's Vineyard Chamber of Commerce** (Beach Rd., Vineyard Haven, tel. 508/693–0085) and pick up a copy of the "Tick-Borne Disease" brochure.

TENNIS

Tennis is very popular on the island, and at all times reservations are strongly recommended. In winter the sport is called "guerrilla tennis," played on private courts with the nets still up and the owners far away—do this at your own risk, naturally.

WATER SPORTS

There's water, water everywhere and plenty to do on, in, and near it. Options include swimming (ocean, ponds, sounds, and a limited number of pools), boating, sailing, kayaking, canoeing, windsurfing, surfing, Jet Skiing, water skiing, and parasailing—or simply floating on a inflatable rubber raft. Martha's Vineyard is ideal for fish wanna-bes. Neophytes can practice windsurfing on the protected waters of the many bays and inlets, while the ocean-side surf provides plenty of action for experts. There are Jet Ski rentals, though the sport is not as popular here as in other regions. Kayakers can put in at a number of landings, whether on the sound, lagoons, or inlets that lead out to larger ponds.

Weather Wise

That old New England saying—"If you don't like the weather, wait a minute"—is even more applicable on a New England island. Those planning outdoor activities should check weather conditions and extended forecasts. Here are several ways to know which way the wind blows:

The Coast Guard recommends the National Weather Service Web site, www.nws.noaa.gov. Also try www.mvy.com, which connects to the weather page of Weather.com.

The island's cable TV Channel 8 reports the weather 24 hours a day. The Weather Channel also reports local conditions, as does the island radio station, WMVY (92.7 FM).

In the event of a hurricane warning (August and September are the most common months here) tune into WMVY, call the Dukes County Emergency Management Agency (EMA; tel. 508/696–6499), contact your town's EMA volunteer director (reached through local town hall), or call the local chapter of the American Red Cross (tel. 508/696–0092).

To rent and operate a motor boat, you have to be at least 12 years old. Between 12 and 17, you need a permit issued by the state after you've completed an 8- to 10-hour course. Anyone over 18 can operate a boat, but it's up to the discretion of the outfitter to determine if you're skilled enough to do so. The rental of personal watercraft—that's the generic name for Jet Skis, Yamaha Wave Runners, and other motorized water scooters—by those ages 16 and 17 requires a valid state-administered safety boating license, obtained after passing a course. Over 18, you're good to go.

Several hotels have in-ground swimming pools; the indoor pool at the Tisbury Inn in Vineyard Haven is the only one non-guests can pay a day rate to use.

The island has become a very popular destination for kayakers, whether they bring their own or rent them on the island, with easy-to-reach put-ins that allow them to glide to some areas unreachable by any other means. Most rental outlets offer guided tours; some give lessons. One outfitter, Kayaks of Martha's Vineyard, leads a couple of weekend trips the end of the summer across Vineyard Sound to Penikese Island in the Elizabeth Islands as a benefit for the Penikese Island School for adolescent boys.

For sailors young and old, the nonprofit Sail Martha's Vineyard offers lessons, as do Island Sailing Schools of Martha's Vineyard, Winds Up!, and the three private island yacht clubs in Vineyard Haven, Edgartown, and Oak Bluffs.

DOWN-ISLAND

VINEYARD HAVEN (TISBURY)
Biking

Beach Road Rentals (95 Beach Rd., tel. 508/693–3793) rents bikes, mountain bikes, hybrids, tandems, and kids' bikes. Scooters and mopeds are also available.

Cycle Works (351 State Rd., tel. 508/693–6966), along with renting all variety of bikes, also has an excellent repair shop.

Martha's Bike Rentals (4 Lagoon Pond Rd., at Five Corners, tel. 508/693–6593) rents bicycles, helmets, baby seats, and trailer bikes that attach to the rear of adult bikes to carry kids. It also handles repairs and will deliver and pick up your bike free anywhere on the island.

Martha's Vineyard Strictly Bikes (24 Union St., tel. 508/693–0782) rents a variety of bicycles and baby trailers. It also sells bikes and does repairs.

Boating

Wind's Up! (199 Beach Rd., tel. 508/693–4252 or 508/693–4340) rents day sailers, catamarans, surfboards, sea kayaks, canoes, and Sunfish, as well as Windsurfers and boogie boards, and offers lessons.

Martha's Vineyard Parasailing, Water Skiing and Jet Skiing (Pier 44 Marina, Beach Rd., tel. 508/693–2838) offers equipment for tons of water sports, including wake boarding, knee boarding, and tubing. New are Yamaha Wave Runners (like Jet Skis but you sit down).

Golf

The semiprivate **Mink Meadows Golf Club** (Golf Club Rd. at Franklin St., tel. 508/693–0600), on West Chop, has nine holes and ocean views. Reservations must be made 48 hours in advance.

Health and Fitness Clubs

The **Health Club at the Tisbury Inn** (9 Main St., tel. 508/693–7400) has Lifecycle, Nautilus, Universal, and StairMaster machines; bikes; free-weight rooms; tanning facilities; aerobics classes; and personal trainers. The club also has a large heated pool, a hot tub, and a sauna. Short-term memberships, from one day to a month, are available.

Fitness Firm of Martha's Vineyard (155 State Rd., tel. 508/693–5533) has Lifecycle bikes and Precor EFX cross-training and Icarian strength equipment, as well as a full array of free weights. There are personal trainers on staff. Day, weekly, monthly, and yearly memberships are available.

Miniature Golf

Island Cove Mini Golf (State Rd., tel. 508/693–2611) offers an 18-hole course with bridges, a cave, rocklike obstacles, sand traps, and a stream that powers a water mill. Next door is Mad Martha's, where the winners can be treated to ice cream.

Tennis

The public clay courts on Church Street are open in season only and charge $8 for singles and $10 for doubles between July 1 and Labor Day. There are two asphalt courts on Lake Street (heading toward Lake Tashmoo, to the left of a large rock painted blue at the curve), available for free on a first-come, first-served basis Monday and Wednesday when town recreation programs are not under way.

OAK BLUFFS
Biking

Anderson's (Circuit Ave. Ext., tel. 508/693–9346), on the harbor, rents several different styles of bicycle.

DeBettencourt's (Circuit Ave. Ext., tel. 508/693–0011) rents bikes, mopeds, scooters, and Jeeps.

Harbor Rentals (Circuit Ave. Ext., tel. 508/693–1300) rents several different types of bicycle, as well as mopeds.

Ride-On Mopeds and Bikes (Circuit Ave. Ext., tel. 508/693–2076 or 508/693–4498) rents bicycles and mopeds.

Sun 'n' Fun (28 Lake Ave., tel. 508/693–5457) rents bikes, cars, and Jeeps.

Boating

Vineyard Boat Rentals (Dockside Marketplace, Oak Bluffs Harbor, tel. 508/693–8476) rents Boston Whalers, Yamaha Wave Runner personal watercraft, and kayaks.

Martha's Vineyard Parasailing, Water Skiing and Jet Skiing (Dockside Marina, tel. 508/693–2838) offers equipment for tons of water sports, including wake boarding, knee boarding, and tubing. New are Yamaha Wave Runners.

Fishing

Dick's Bait and Tackle (New York Ave., tel. 508/693–7669) rents gear, sells accessories and bait, and keeps a current copy of the fishing regulations.

The party boat *Skipper* (Oak Bluffs Harbor, tel. 508/693–1238) leaves for deep-sea fishing trips out of Oak Bluffs Harbor in July and August. Reservations are mandatory.

Health and Fitness Clubs

Muscle Discipline (29 Kennebec Ave., tel. 508/693–5096) has Lifecycle, Nautilus, StairMaster, treadmill, and cross-training machines and free weights. All staff are certified trainers. Eight TVs are located throughout the gym. Daily, weekly, monthly, and three-month summer memberships are available.

Golf

Farm Neck Golf Club (County Rd., tel. 508/693–3057), a semiprivate club on marsh-rimmed Sengekontacket Pond, has 18 holes in a championship layout and a driving range. Reservations are required 48 hours in advance.

Windfarm Golf Driving Range (203 Edgartown–Vineyard Haven Rd., tel. 508/693–4842) is open daily for duffers in need of a few practice swings. Tees are covered for rainy-day play, and lessons are available.

Ice-Skating

Martha's Vineyard Arena (Edgartown–Vineyard Haven Rd., tel. 508/693–4438) is open mid-July–March. Open public skating is from noon to 1:30 PM weekdays, 5 to 6:20 PM weekends.

In-Line Skating

Island Outfitters (1 Post Office Sq., tel. 508/693–5003) is a clothing store whose owner rents in-line skates because he loves to skate himself. K2 inline skates are available for one or three-day rentals or on a weekly basis. Instruction is included in the rental price.

Scuba Diving

Vineyard waters hold a number of sunken ships, among them several schooners and freighters off East Chop and Aquinnah. Visibility is decent, though the water clarity isn't in the same league as that of the Caribbean. Guided dives are the norm.

Vineyard Scuba (110 S. Circuit Ave., tel. 508/693–0288) has diving information and equipment rentals and is the only full-service dive shop on the island. Certification classes are given; they can also arrange for dive guides.

Tennis

Tennis is very popular on the island, and at all times reservations are strongly recommended. **Farm Neck Golf Club** (County Rd., tel. 508/693–9728) is a semiprivate club with four clay tennis courts, lessons, and a pro shop. It's open mid-April through mid-November; reservations are required.

Island Country Club Tennis (Beach Rd., tel. 508/693–6574) is a semiprivate club with three Har-Tru courts and a pro shop. It's open May–Columbus Day.

Hard-surface courts in **Niantic Park** (tel. 508/693–6535) cost a small fee and are open year-round.

EDGARTOWN
Biking

Several bike paths lace through the Edgartown area, including a path to Oak Bluffs that has a spectacular view of Sengekontacket Pond on one side and Nantucket Sound on the other.

Edgartown Bicycles (Upper Main St., tel. 508/627–9008) offers a full array of rentals and repairs.

R. W. Cutler Bike (1 Main St., tel. 508/627–4052) rents and repairs all types of bicycles.

Triangle (Upper Main St., tel. 508/627–7099) has bicycles available for rent.

Wheelhappy (8 S. Water St., tel. 508/627–5928) rents bicycles and will deliver them to you.

Boating

Gold Coast Para-sailing, Ocean Kayak & Race Boat Rides (Dock St., at the docks behind Seafood Shanty, tel. 508/693–3330) offers parasailing for all ages; ocean kayaks for one or two by the hour, day, or week; and 40-minute race-boat trips, at 80 mph, for up to six people at a time.

Fishing

The annual **Martha's Vineyard Striped Bass & Bluefish Derby** (Box 2101, Edgartown 02539, tel. 508/693–0728), from mid-September to mid-October, offers daily, weekly, and derby prizes for striped bass, bluefish, bonito, and false albacore catches, from boat or shore. The derby is a real Vineyard tradition, cause for loyal devotion among locals who drop everything to cast their lines at all hours of day and night in search of that prizewinning whopper. Avid fisherfolk come from all over the rest of the country, too, to cast their fates to the fishing gods.

Big Eye Charters (tel. 508/627–3649) offers fishing charters that leave from Edgartown Harbor.

Coop's Bait and Tackle (147 W. Tisbury Rd., tel. 508/627–3909) sells accessories and bait, rents fishing gear, and keeps a current listing of fishing regulations.

Larry's Tackle Shop (141 Main St., tel. 508/627–5088) rents gear and sells accessories and bait and has a copy of the fishing regulations.

Hooked on the Derby

If there's a spiritual pilgrimage for fishermen, it's probably the annual **Martha's Vineyard Striped Bass & Bluefish Derby.** Since it's start in 1946, it has evoked near religious reaction among those to whom hooking a striper, bluefish, bonito, or false albacore ranks right up there with seeing a burning bush.

Why? "First, Martha's Vineyard is a beautiful place to fish," says Derby board member and Martha's Vineyard Times fishing columnist Nelson Sigelman. "Second, with so many categories, everyone has an opportunity to win. And it's one of the largest shore tournaments in the country."

The categories are for both boat and shore fishing, with daily and overall prizes for winners—men, women, senior citizens, and juniors. And this isn't just for the lifelong fanatics. There's even a free kid's mini-derby, a Saturday morning contest held in September at the steamship wharf in Oak Bluffs.

But the real magic is not in connecting with a big one. It's connecting with a fellow fisher that brings the addicts back every year."There you are at 2 AM out on Cape Pogue bar having a conversation with someone you never met before, and then meeting that same person year after year—same time, same place—until you become fast friends," says Sigelman.

No wonder the event, held from mid-September to mid-October, attracts some 2,000 entrants from around the world who compete for cash and other prizes, including the grand prize of a Boston Whaler. A portion of the proceeds from derby entry fees goes to support scholastic scholarships for island students.

And while no true fisherman will reveal his or her favorite spot, in true fishing fashion they will all gladly tell you about the "one that got away"— the one that would have won them the derby grand prize.

The **Slapshot II** (tel. 508/627–8087) is available for fishing charters from Edgartown Harbor.

Health and Fitness Clubs

Triangle Fitness (Post Office Square at the Triangle, tel. 508/627–3393) has stair climbers, stationary bikes, elliptical cross-trainers, and Body Master weightlifting equipment; personal trainers are available. There are also classes in aerobics, spinning, yoga, conditioning, step, karate, and kick boxing. Daily, weekly, monthly, and yearly memberships are available.

Recreation Areas

Edgartown Recreation Area (Robinson Rd., tel. 508/627–7574) has five tennis courts, a basketball court, a softball field, a roller hockey court, a picnic area, and playground equipment. Activities (published in local papers) include tennis round-robins, softball and basketball games, arts and crafts, and rainy-day events. Also see the "Island Recreation" section of the *Vineyard Gazette*'s calendar for open Frisbee, rugby, and other games.

Tennis

Reservations are usually necessary for the hard-surface courts at the **Edgartown Recreation Area** (☞ *above*). There's a small fee, and the courts are open year-round.

UP-ISLAND

WEST TISBURY
Horseback Riding

Arrowhead Farm (Indian Hill Rd., tel. 508/693–8831) offers riding lessons for adults and children year-round, as well as children's summer horsemanship programs. The farm has an indoor ring and leases horses but does not offer trail rides.

Manuel F. Correllus State Forest (access off Barnes Rd., Old County Rd., and Edgartown–West Tisbury Rd.) is laced with horse trails open to the public, but it has no stables.

Crow Hollow Farm (Tiah's Cove Rd., tel. 508/696–4554) offers trail rides for experienced riders only, plus lessons and clinics.

Red Pony Farm (off Edgartown–West Tisbury Rd., tel. 508/693–3788) offers trail rides for experienced riders only. A bed-and-breakfast package includes a room above the barn plus a weekend of riding and lessons for all levels.

Iron Hill Farm (off Edgartown–Vineyard Haven Rd., at entrance to Thimble Farm, tel. 508/292–0719) offers trail and pony rides as well as lessons.

Tennis

Stop by to reserve hard-surface courts at the grammar school on Old County Road in West Tisbury. There is a small fee for using the courts, which are open year-round.

On rainy days you can head to the **Vineyard Tennis Center** (22 Airport Rd., tel. 508/696–8000) at the entrance to the airport. For a fee you can play at the indoor courts until 10 PM. A new fitness club at the tennis center has Precor EFX and Cybex circuit equipment, as well as free weights.

CHILMARK
Fishing

Bass Ackwards (Basin Rd., Menemsha Harbor, tel. 508/645–2915) specializes in striped bass charters.

Flashy Lady Charters (Menemsha Harbor, tel. 508/645–2462) offers all kinds of charters.

Galatea Charters (Coast Guard dock, Menemsha Harbor, tel. 508/645–9238) offers fly fishing and light tackle fishing for bass, bluefish, bonito, and false albacore.

Distance Conversion Chart

Kilometers/Miles

To change kilometers (km) to miles (mi), multiply km by .621.
To change mi to km, multiply mi by 1.61.

km to mi	mi to km
1 = .62	1 = 1.6
2 = 1.2	2 = 3.2
3 = 1.9	3 = 4.8
4 = 2.5	4 = 6.4
5 = 3.1	5 = 8.1
6 = 3.7	6 = 9.7
7 = 4.3	7 = 11.3
8 = 5.0	8 = 12.9

Meters/Feet

To change meters (m) to feet (ft), multiply m by 3.28.
To change ft to m, multiply ft by .305.

m to ft	ft to m
1 = 3.3	1 = .30
2 = 6.6	2 = .61
3 = 9.8	3 = .92
4 = 13.1	4 = 1.2
5 = 16.4	5 = 1.5
6 = 19.7	6 = 1.8
7 = 23.0	7 = 2.1
8 = 26.2	8 = 2.4

Menemsha Blues Charters (Basin Rd., Menemsha Harbor, tel. 508/645–3778) offers bass, bluefish, and bonita charters out of Menemsha.

North Shore Charters (Menemsha Harbor, tel. 508/645–2993) has boats for charter.

Sortie Charters (Basin Rd., Menemsha Harbor, tel. 508/645–3015) offers a variety of charters.

AQUINNAH

Conomo Charters (10 Old South Rd., tel. 508/645–9278), under Captain Brian Vanderhoop, leads striped bass and bluefish trips.

Tomahawk Charters (tel. 508/645–3201), with Captain Buddy Vanderhoop at the helm, specializes in striped-bass fishing trips as well as bluefish, tuna, bonita, and sharks. Captain Lisa Vanderhoop also leads fishing charters especially for kids.

Menemsha Creek Charters (tel. 508/645–3511), run by Captain Hugh Taylor, leads two trips a day aboard the catamaran *Arabella* for swimming and picnicking for up to 40 people at a time. Day trips to Cuttyhunk depart at 10:30 AM and return at 3:30 PM; there are daily sunset cruises, too.

The cliffs of Aquinnah shimmer in the afternoon sun. The hike to the beach was worth it, you think to yourself—they look so much larger here than from the observation deck, great, looming towers of ochre, gold, green, and black, the legendary home of native Wampanoag gods. As you walk down the beach, a man in front of you stands at the base of the cliffs, gazing up, mesmerized. Ten minutes later you pass him, still staring, and a few minutes later you discreetly glance back. He hasn't moved.

In This Chapter

By Karl Luntta

here and there

CHARACTERIZING MARTHA'S VINEYARD is a bit like characterizing the taste of milk; it's a complete, and unique, experience unlike any other. The three towns that compose Down-Island (the east end of Martha's Vineyard)—Vineyard Haven, Oak Bluffs, and Edgartown—are the most popular and the most populated. Here you'll find the ferry docks, the shops, and a concentration of things to do and see, including the centuries-old houses and churches that document the island's history. A stroll through any one of these towns allows you to look into the past while enjoying the pleasures of the present.

However, much of what makes the Vineyard special is found in its rural reaches, in the agricultural heart of the island and the largely undeveloped lands south and west of the Vineyard Haven–to–Edgartown line known as Up-Island. Country roads meander through woods and tranquil farmland, and dirt side roads lead past crystalline ponds, abandoned cranberry bogs, and conservation lands. In Chilmark, West Tisbury, and Aquinnah, nature lovers, writers, artists, and others have established close, ongoing summer communities. In winter, the isolation and bitter winds generally send even year-round Vineyarders from their Up-Island homes to places in the cozier Down-Island towns.

Numbers in the text correspond to numbers in the margin and on the Vineyard Haven, Oak Bluffs, Edgartown, and Up-Island maps.

DOWN-ISLAND

VINEYARD HAVEN (TISBURY)

3½ mi west of Oak Bluffs, 8 mi northwest of Edgartown by the inland route.

Most people call this town Vineyard Haven for the name of the port where the ferry pulls in, but its official name is Tisbury. Not as high-toned as Edgartown nor as honky-tonk as Oak Bluffs, Vineyard Haven blends the past and the present with a touch of the bohemian. Settled in the mid-1600s when the island's first governor-to-be purchased rights to the land from local Wampanoags, it is the busiest year-round community on Martha's Vineyard. Visitors arriving here step off the ferry right into the bustle of the harbor, a block from the shops and restaurants of Main Street.

If you need to stock up on maps or information on the island, ❶ **Martha's Vineyard Chamber of Commerce** is a good place to get your bearings. The office is around the corner from the steamship terminal (where you'll find a small information booth, open daily 8–8 in season) on Beach Road. *24 Beach Rd., tel. 508/ 693–0085. Weekdays 9–5 (plus abbreviated weekend hours in season).*

....

NEED A BREAK? | The **Black Dog Bakery's** (11 Water St., tel. 508/693–4786) delicious breads, pastries, and quick-lunch items are simply not to be missed—it's a popular stop for good reason.

....

❷ The stately, neoclassic 1844 **Association Hall** (51 Spring St., tel. 508/696–4200) houses the town hall and the **Katharine Cornell Memorial Theatre,** created in part with funds that Cornell (1898–1974)—one of America's foremost stage actresses in the 1920s, '30s, and '40s and a longtime summer resident—donated in her will. The walls of the theater on the second floor are painted with murals depicting whaling expeditions and a Native American gathering, while the ceiling resembles a blue sky with seagulls overhead. Island artist Stan Murphy painted the murals on the occasion of the town's tercentenary in 1971. The theater holds performances of plays, concerts, and dances.

❸ At the **Centre Street Cemetery** (Centre St., between William and Franklin Sts.), tall pine trees shade grave markers dating as far back as 1817. Some stones are simple gray slate slabs, while others are carved with such motifs as the death's-head—a skull, common on tombstones of the era. A more recent grave is that of the actress Katharine Cornell, who died in 1974 and whose largesse helped build the theater (housed in the Association Hall; ☞ *above*) named for her.

A stroll down **William Street,** a quiet stretch of white picket fences and Greek Revival houses, many of them built for prosperous sea captains, lets you imagine the town as it was in the 19th century. Now a part of a National Historic District, the street was spared when the Great Fire of 1883 claimed much of the old whaling and fishing town.

❹ Built in 1829, the **Old Schoolhouse Building** was the first town school and today houses the Vineyard Seaman's Society and Bethel Maritime Collection. You can view items brought back from voyages during whaling days, including Inuit and Polynesian tools, as well as antique musical instruments, clothing, and the school records of 19th-century schoolchildren. Out front, the **Liberty Pole** was erected by the Daughters of the American Revolution in honor of three patriotic girls who blew up the town's liberty pole in 1776 to prevent it from being taken for use on a British warship. The museum occasionally experiences staffing problems, so call for current opening times. *110 Main St., tel. 508/693–9317. $2. Mid-June–mid-Sept., Tues.–Fri. and Sun. noon–4.*

❺ For a little relaxation, try the tree-shaded benches in **William Barry Owen Park** (off Owen Park Rd.), a lovely spot for a picnic and for summer concerts held at the bandstand. At the end of the lawn

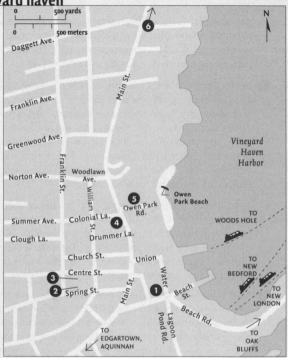

Association Hall, 2

Old Schoolhouse Building, 4

Centre Street Cemetery, 3

Owen Park, 5

Martha's Vineyard Chamber of Commerce, 1

West Chop, 6

is a public beach with a swing set and a close-up view of the boats sailing in and out of the harbor. In the 19th century this harbor was one of the busiest ports in the world, welcoming thousands of vessels each year. Lighthouses still stand at the headlands—West Chop in Vineyard Haven and East Chop in Oak Bluffs—to help bring ships safely into port.

❻ Beautiful and green, **West Chop** retains its exclusive air and claims some of the island's most distinguished residents. This area, as well as East Chop across the harbor, was largely settled in the late 19th to early 20th century, when the very rich from Boston and Newport built expansive bluff-top "summer cottages." The shingle-style houses, characterized by broad gable ends, dormers, and natural shingle siding that weathers to gray, were meant to eschew pretense, though they were sometimes gussied up with a turret or two. A 2-mi walk, drive, or bike ride along Vineyard Haven's Main Street—which becomes increasingly residential on the way—will take you there.

One of two lighthouses that mark the opening to the harbor, the 52-ft white-and-black **West Chop Lighthouse** (W. Chop Rd. [Main St.]) was built in 1838 of brick to replace an 1817 wood building. It has been moved back twice from the edge of the eroding bluff. (It is not open to the public.) Just beyond the lighthouse, on the point, is a scenic overlook with a landscaped area and benches.

West Chop Woods is an 85-acre conservation area with marked walking trails through pitch pine and oak. The area is just south and west of the West Chop lighthouse, with entrances and parking spots on Main Street and Franklin Street.

Martha's Vineyard Shellfish Group grows seed clams, scallops, and oysters to stock lagoons and beds throughout the county. From spring through fall, tours of the solar shellfish hatchery on Lagoon Pond in Vineyard Haven can be arranged with advance notice. *Weaver La., tel. 508/693–0391. $5 donation suggested. Call for appointment.*

oak bluffs

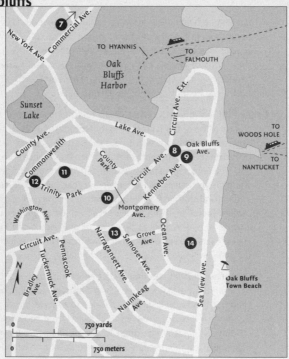

New York Ave.

Commercial Ave.

7

TO HYANNIS

TO FALMOUTH

Oak Bluffs Harbor

Circuit Ave. Ext.

Sunset Lake

Lake Ave.

County Ave.

Commonwealth

County Park

Circuit Ave.

Oak Bluffs Ave.

8 **9**

TO WOODS HOLE

TO NANTUCKET

11

12 Trinity Park

Kennebec Ave.

10

Montgomery Ave.

Washington Ave.

Ocean Ave.

Circuit Ave.

Pennacook

13

Grove Ave.

Samoset Ave.

14

Naumkeag Ave.

Sea View Ave.

Oak Bluffs Town Beach

Narragansett Ave.

Tuckermuck Ave.

Bradley Ave.

N

0   750 yards

0   750 meters

OAK BLUFFS

3½ mi east of Vineyard Haven, 6 mi northwest of Edgartown, 22 mi northeast of Aquinnah.

Purchased from the Wampanoags in the 1660s, Oak Bluffs was a farming community that did not come into its own until the 1830s, when Methodists began holding summer revivalist meetings in a stand of oaks known as Wesleyan Grove, named for Methodism's founder, John Wesley. As the camp meetings caught on, attendees built small cottages in place of tents. Then the general population took notice and the area became a popular summer vacation spot. Hotels, a dance hall, a roller-skating rink, and other shops and amusements were built to accommodate the flocks of summer visitors.

Today Circuit Avenue is the center of action in Oak Bluffs, the address of most of the town's shops, bars, and restaurants. Oak Bluffs Harbor, once the setting for a number of grand hotels—the 1879 Wesley Hotel on Lake Avenue is the last of them—is still crammed with gingerbread-trimmed guest houses and food and souvenir joints. With its whimsical cottages, long beachfront, and funky shops, the small town is more high-spirited than haute, more fun than refined.

East Chop is one of two points of land that jut out into the Nantucket–Vineyard sound, creating the sheltered harbor at Vineyard Haven and some fine views. From Oak Bluffs, take East Chop Drive, or you can loop out to the point on your way from Vineyard Haven by taking Highland Drive off Beach Road after crossing the drawbridge.

❼ The **East Chop Lighthouse** was built of cast iron in 1876 to replace an 1828 tower—used as part of a semaphore system of visual signaling between the island and Boston—that burned down. The 40-ft structure stands high atop a 79-ft bluff with spectacular views of Nantucket Sound. East Chop is one of three island lighthouses open to the public. *E. Chop Dr., tel. 508/627–4441. $2. Late June–late Sept., 1 hr before sunset–1 hr after sunset.*

8 The **information booth** will help you get your bearings and point the way to the not-to-be-missed spots in Oak Bluffs, with some good tips for gingerbread-trim lovers. *Corner of Lake and Oak Bluffs Aves., tel. 508/693–4266. Mid-May–mid-Oct., daily 9–5.*

9 A National Historic Landmark, the **Flying Horses Carousel** is the nation's oldest continuously operating carousel. Handcrafted in 1876 (the horses have real horse hair and glass eyes), the ride offers children a taste of entertainment from a TV-free era. While waiting in line (the carousel can get crowded on summer evenings or rainy days, but the wait is rarely longer than 20 minutes or so—avoid the crunch by going early in the day), you can munch on popcorn or cotton candy or slurp a slush. The waiting area has a number of arcade games. *Oak Bluffs Ave., tel. 508/693–9481. Rides $1; $8 for a book of 10. Memorial Day–Labor Day, daily 10–10; Easter–Memorial Day, weekends 10–5; Labor Day–Columbus Day, weekdays 11–4:30, weekends 10–5.*

. . . .

NEED A BREAK? The **Coop de Ville** (Dockside Marketplace, Oak Bluffs Harbor, tel. 508/693–3420) often teems with people eager to sample the delectables from the raw bar and the simple fried seafood. Eat out on the patio deck overlooking the water—the oysters are fantastic. It's open May through Columbus Day.

Some like it sweet, and with all its homemade ice cream, the long-standing local joint **Mad Martha's** (117 Circuit Ave., tel. 508/693–9151) is just the place for a sweet tooth. There's a great jukebox, too. It's open from May through August and stays open until midnight in July and August.

. . . .

★ **10** Don't miss a look at **Oak Bluffs Camp Ground,** a 34-acre warren of streets tightly packed with more than 300 Carpenter Gothic Victorian cottages with wedding-cake trim, gaily painted in pastels. As you wander through this fairy-tale setting, imagine it on a balmy summer evening, lit by the warm glow of hundreds of Japanese paper lanterns hung from every cottage porch. This describes the scene on Illumination Night at the end of the Camp Meeting season—attended these days by some fourth- and fifth-generation cottagers. Attendees mark the occasion as they have for more than a century, with lights, song, and open houses for families and friends. Note that because of overwhelming crowds of onlookers in seasons past, the date is not announced until the week before. *Off Circuit Ave.*

⑪ The **Tabernacle,** an impressive open-air structure of iron and wood at the center of Trinity Park, is the original site of the Methodist services. On Wednesdays at 8 PM in season, visitors are invited to join in on an old-time community sing-along. If you know tunes like "The Erie Canal" or just want to listen in, drop by the Tabernacle and take a seat. Music books are available for a donation. Sunday services are held in summer at 9:30 AM. The 1878 **Trinity Methodist Church** also stands in the park and is open for visits during daylight hours (no tours however) and, of course, for services on Sunday.

For a glimpse at life in Cottage City during its heyday, visit the ⑫ **Cottage Museum,** in an 1868 Creamsicle-hue cottage near the Tabernacle. The two-story museum exhibits cottage furnishings from the early days, including photographs, hooked rugs, quilts, and old Bibles. The gift shop offers Victorian and nautical items. *1 Trinity Park, tel. 508/693–7784. $1 donation requested. Mid-June–Sept., Mon.–Sat. 10–4.*

⑬ An octagonal, nonsectarian house of worship, **Union Chapel** was constructed in 1870 for the Cottage City resort folk who lived outside the Camp Ground's 7-ft-high fence. In summer, concerts are held here, as are 10 AM Sunday services. *Corner of Kennebec and Samoset Aves., tel. 508/693–1093.*

⑭ A long stretch of green facing the sea, **Ocean Park** fronts a crescent of large shingle-style cottages with numerous turrets, breezy porches, and pastel facades. Band concerts take place at the gazebo here on summer nights, and in August the park hosts

edgartown

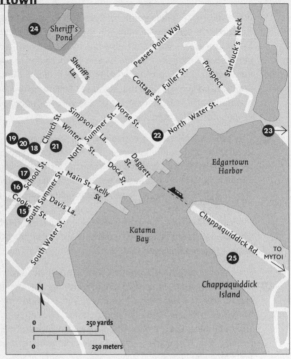

hordes of island families and visitors for a grand fireworks display over the ocean. *Sea View Ave.*

EDGARTOWN

6 mi southeast of Oak Bluffs, 9 mi southeast of Vineyard Haven via Beach Rd., 8½ mi east of West Tisbury.

Edgartown has long been the Vineyard's toniest spot. Ever since Thomas Mayhew, Jr., landed here in 1642 as the Vineyard's first governor, the town has served as the county seat. Plenty of settlers inhabited the area, making it the island's first Colonial settlement, but the town was not officially named until 1652. First called Great Harbour, it was renamed for political reasons some 30 years later, after the three-year-old son of the Duke of York.

Once a well-to-do whaling port, Edgartown has managed to preserve the elegance of that wealthy era. Lining the streets are 18th- and 19th-century sea captains' houses, many painted white with black shutters, set among well-manicured gardens and lawns. There are plenty of shops here, as well as other sights and activities to occupy the crowds who walk the streets. A stroll is definitely the best way to absorb it all.

To orient yourself historically before making your way around town, stop off at a complex of buildings and lawn exhibits that constitutes
★ ⓯ the **Vineyard Museum and Oral History Center.** The opening hours and admission listed below apply to all the buildings and exhibits—including the Thomas Cooke House, the Francis Foster Museum, the Capt. Francis Pease House, and the Carriage Shed— unless otherwise noted. The museum, administered by the Martha's Vineyard Historical Society, sells an excellent Edgartown walking-tour booklet full of anecdotes and the history of the people who have lived in the old houses over the past three centuries. You can purchase it at the entrance gatehouse in summer or at the library in winter. *Corner of Cooke and School Sts., tel. 508/627–4441. $6. Mid-June–mid-Oct., Tues.–Sat. 10–5; mid-Oct.– mid-June, Wed.–Fri. 1–4, Sat. 10–4.*

The one Vineyard Museum property open mid-June to mid-October only is the **Thomas Cooke House** (School St., tel. 508/627–4441), set in the 1765 home of a customs collector. The house itself is part of the display, evoking the past with its low doorways, wide-board floors, original raised-panel woodwork with fluted pilasters, and hearths in the summer and winter kitchens. Docents conduct tours of the 12 rooms, whose exhibits reveal the island's history with furniture, tools, costumes, portraits, toys, crafts, and various household objects. One room is set up as a 19th-century parlor, illustrating the opulence of the golden age of whaling with such period pieces as a pianoforte. Upstairs are ship models, whaling paraphernalia, old customs documents, and a room tracing the evolution of the Camp Meeting through photographs and objects.

The **Francis Foster Museum** (School St., tel. 508/627–4441) houses a small collection of whaling implements, scrimshaw, navigational instruments, and many old photographs. One interesting exhibit is a collection of 19th-century miniature photographs of 110 Edgartown whaling masters, grouped by family. The **Dale Huntington Reference Library and Foster Maritime Gallery** is also in the building, with genealogical records, rare island books, and ships' logs from the whaling days, as well as some publications for sale.

The **Capt. Francis Pease House** (School St., tel. 508/627–4441), an 1850s Greek Revival, houses a permanent exhibit of Native American, prehistoric, pre-Columbian, and later artifacts, including arrowheads and pottery, plus changing exhibits from the collection. The Children's Gallery presents changing exhibits created by children, and the museum shop sells books, maps, jewelry, and island crafts.

The **Carriage Shed** (School St., tel. 508/627–4441) displays a number of vessels and vehicles, among them a whaleboat, a snazzy 1855 fire engine with stars inlaid in wood, and an 1830 hearse, considerably less ornate than the fire engine. The shed also houses some peculiar gravestones that mark the eternal resting places of an eccentric poet's strangely beloved chickens. In the yard outside are a replica of a 19th-century **brick tryworks,** used to process whale oil from blubber aboard ship, and the 1,008-prism **Fresnel lens** installed in the Aquinnah Lighthouse (☞ Aquinnah, *below*) in 1854 and removed when the light was automated in 1952. Each evening the lens lamp is lighted briefly after sundown. The **tool shed** contains harvesting tools used both on land and at sea in the early 19th century.

⑱ The **Old Whaling Church** (89 Main St., tel. 508/627–8619 for tour), which opened in 1843 as a Methodist church and is now a performing-arts center, is a massive building with a six-column portico, unusual triple-sash windows, and a 92-ft clock tower that can be seen for miles. The simple, graceful interior is brightened by light from 27-ft-tall windows and still contains the original box pews and lectern. Aside from attending performances, you can get inside only if you join one of the historical walking tours offered by Vineyard History Tours (☞ Tour Operators in Practical Information, *below*).

⑲ A truly elegant sight is the graceful **Dr. Daniel Fisher House** (99 Main St.), with a wraparound roof walk and a small front portico with fluted Corinthian columns. It was built in 1840 for one of the island's richest men, who was a doctor, the first president of the Martha's Vineyard National Bank, and the owner of a whale-oil refinery, a spermaceti (whale-oil) candle factory, and a gristmill, among other pursuits. The good doctor came to a portion of his fortune through marriage—as a wedding gift, his generous but presumably eccentric father-in-law presented him with the bride's weight in silver. The house is now used for functions and office space, and you can gain access only on Liz Villard's Vineyard History Tours (☞ Contacts and Resources in Martha's Vineyard A to Z, *below*).

⑳ The island's oldest dwelling is the 1672 **Vincent House.** It was moved to its present location behind the Dr. Daniel Fisher House (☞ *above*) in 1977, restored, and furnished with pieces that date from the 17th to the 19th century. A tour of this weathered-shingle farmhouse takes you along a time-line that starts with the sparse furnishings of the 1600s and ends in a Federal-style parlor of the 1800s. *Main St., tel. 508/627–4440. Museum $3, Museum and tour $7 (includes Old Whaling Church). Late May–Oct., Mon.–Sat. 10–3.*

㉑ A good place to stop for directions or suggestions is the **Edgartown Visitors Center** (Church St., no phone), which offers information, rest rooms, and snacks in season.

NEED A BREAK? If you need a pick-me-up, pop into **Espresso Love** (3 S. Water St., tel. 508/627–9211) for a cappuccino and a homemade raspberry scone or blueberry muffin. If you prefer something cold, the staff makes fruit smoothies. Light lunch fare is also served: bagel sandwiches, soups, and delicious pastries and cookies—all homemade, of course.

The architecturally pristine, much-photographed upper part of North Water Street is lined with many fine captains' houses. There's always an interesting detail on this stretch that you never noticed before—like a widow's walk with a mannequin poised, spyglass in hand, watching for her seafaring husband to return. The 1832 house where this piece of whimsy can be seen stands

㉒ at **86 North Water Street,** which the Society for the Preservation of New England Antiquities maintains as a rental property.

㉓ The **Edgartown Lighthouse,** surrounded by a public beach, offers a great view (but seaweedy bathing). The original light guarding the harbor was built in 1828 and set on a little island made of granite blocks. The island was later connected to the mainland by a bridge. By the time the 1938 hurricane made a new light necessary, sand had filled in the gap between the island and the mainland. The current white cast-iron tower was floated by barge from Ipswich, Massachusetts, in 1938. This area, called Starbuck's Neck, is a good place to wander about and take in views of the ocean, harbor, a little bay, and moorland. *Off N. Water St. $2. Late June–late Sept., 1 hr before sunset–1 hr after sunset.*

A pleasant walking trail circles an old ice pond at the center of
24 **Sheriff's Meadow Sanctuary** (Planting Field Way, tel. 508/693–
5207), 17 acres of marsh, woodland, and meadow. One of the
area's many wildlife preserves, Sheriff's Meadow contains a
variety of habitats.

★ ☙ The Vineyard's conservation areas are a good way to get acquainted
with local flora and fauna. The 350-acre **Felix Neck Wildlife
Sanctuary,** a Massachusetts Audubon Society preserve 3 mi out
of Edgartown toward Oak Bluffs and Vineyard Haven, has 6 mi of
hiking trails traversing marshland, fields, oak woods, seashore,
and waterfowl and reptile ponds. Nesting ospreys and barn owls
also call the sanctuary home. A full schedule of events unfolds
throughout the year, including sunset hikes along the beach,
explorations of the salt marsh, stargazing, snake or bird walks,
snorkeling, canoeing, and more, all led by trained naturalists. An
exhibit center has trail maps, aquariums, snake cages, and a gift
shop. A bit of summer fun and learning experience combined, the
sanctuary's **Fern & Feather Day Camp** is a great way for children
to learn about wildlife, plants, and the stars. It offers one- or two-
week summer sessions that include overnight camping expeditions.
Early registration is advised and begins in February. *Off Edgartown–
Vineyard Haven Rd., tel. 508/627–4850. $3. Center June–Sept., daily 8–
4; Oct.–May, Tues.–Sun. 9–4. Trails daily sunrise–7 PM.*

CHAPPAQUIDDICK ISLAND
25 *6 mi southeast of Oak Bluffs, across the bay from Edgartown.*

A sparsely populated islet with a great number of nature
preserves, Chappaquiddick Island makes for a pleasant day trip
or bike ride on a sunny day. If you are interested in covering a lot
of it, cycling is the best way to go. The island is actually
connected to the Vineyard by a long sand spit from South Beach
in Katama—a spectacular 2¾-mi walk if you have the energy. If
not, the On Time ferry (☞ *Boat and Ferry Travel in Practical
Information, below*) makes the short trip from Edgartown across

from 7 AM to midnight in season. The ferry departs every five minutes or so but posts no schedule, thereby earning its name—technically, it cannot be late.

The Land Bank's 41-acre **Brine's Pond** (off Chappaquiddick Rd.) is a popular, scenic picnicking spot. Mown grasses surround a serpentine pond with an island in its center and a woodland backdrop behind—a truly lovely setting.

★ The Trustees of Reservations' 14-acre **Mytoi** preserve is a quiet, Japanese-inspired garden with a creek-fed pool, spanned by a bridge and rimmed with Japanese maples, azaleas, bamboo, and irises. The garden was created in 1958 by a private citizen. Restroom facilities are available. *Dike Rd., ⅕ mi from intersection with Chappaquiddick Rd., tel. 508/693-7662. Free. Daily sunrise–sunset.*

At the end of Dike Road is **Dike Bridge,** infamous as the scene of the 1969 accident in which a young woman died in a car driven by Ted Kennedy. The rickety bridge has been replaced, after having been dismantled in 1991, but for ecological reasons, vehicle access over it is limited. There is a ranger station on the bridge that is manned June to September. The **Cape Poge Wildlife Refuge** (☞ below), which includes the spectacular **East Beach** and the **Cape Poge Light,** is across the bridge. *End of Dike Rd., tel. 508/627-3599. Walk-on $3 June–Sept., free rest of yr. Daily sunrise–sunset.*

The **Poucha Pond Reservation,** near the southeast corner of the island, encompasses 99 acres of varied environments. Its trails wander among shady pitch pine and oak forests and around a marshy pond on onetime farmland. One trail end has a great view of the pond, Dike Bridge, and the East Beach dunes in the distance. Bring binoculars for the birds—terns, various herons, gulls, plovers—and repellent for the mosquitoes. *4 mi from Chappaquiddick ferry landing, tel. 508/627-7141. Free. Daily sunrise–sunset.*

A conglomeration of habitats where you can swim, walk, fish, or just sit and enjoy the surroundings, the **Cape Poge Wildlife Refuge** (east end of Dike Rd., 3 mi from the Chappaquiddick ferry landing), on the easternmost shore of Chappaquiddick Island, is more than 6 square mi of wilderness. Its dunes, woods, cedar thickets, moors, salt marshes, ponds, tidal flats, and barrier beach serve as an important migration stopover and nesting area for numerous sea and shore birds. The best way to get to the refuge is as part of a naturalist-led **Jeep drive** (tel. 508/627–3599). You can also get there from Wasque Reservation (☞ *below*) on the south shore of the island. You'll need a four-wheel-drive vehicle to do that, and to get to much of the acreage. The Trustees of Reservations requires an annual permit ($90–$110) for a four-wheel drive, available on-site or through Coop's Bait and Tackle (☞ Outdoor Activities and Sports *in* Edgartown, *above*).

★ The 200-acre **Wasque Reservation** (pronounced *wayce*-kwee), mostly a vast beach, connects Chappaquiddick "Island" with the mainland of the Vineyard in Katama, closing off the south end of Katama Bay. You can fish, sunbathe, take the trail by Swan Pond, walk to the island's southeasternmost tip at Wasque Point, or dip into the surf—with caution, due to strong currents. **Wasque Beach** is accessed by a flat boardwalk with benches overlooking the west end of Swan Pond. It's a pretty walk skirting the pond, with ocean views on one side and poles for osprey nests on the other. Atop a bluff is a pine-shaded picnic grove with a spectacular, practically 180-degree panorama. Below, Swan Pond teems with bird life, including the requisite swans, in the surrounding marsh and beach grasses. Beyond that lie beach, sky, and boat-dotted sea. From the grove, a long boardwalk leads down amid the grasses to **Wasque Point,** a prime surf-casting spot for bluefish and stripers. Rest rooms and drinking water are available. *Located at east end of Wasque Rd., 5 mi from Chappaquiddick ferry landing, tel. 508/627–7260. Cars $3, plus $3 per adult, Memorial Day–mid-Sept.; free rest of yr. Property 24 hrs. Gatehouse Memorial Day–Columbus Day, daily 9–5.*

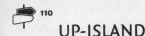
UP-ISLAND

WEST TISBURY

26 6½ mi southwest of Vineyard Haven, 12 mi northeast of Aquinnah.

Founded in the 1670s by settlers from Edgartown, among them the son of Myles Standish and the son-in-law of the Mayflower Aldens, West Tisbury was known for its first 200 Westernized years simply as Tisbury. Among the settlement's advantages over Down-Island outposts, most important was a strong-flowing stream that ran into a pond, creating a perfect mill site—a rarity on the Vineyard. Farming, especially sheep farming, became Tisbury's mainstay.

West Tisbury retains its rural appeal and maintains its agricultural tradition at several active horse and produce farms. The town center looks very much the small New England village, complete with a white, steepled church. Half the 5,146-acre Manuel F. Correllus State Forest lies within the town limits.

The weekly **West Tisbury Farmers' Market**—Massachusetts' largest—is held Wednesdays and Saturdays in summer at the 1859 **Old Agricultural Hall** (South Rd., tel. 508/693–9549), near the town hall. The colorful stands overflow with fresh produce, most of it organic—a refreshing return to life before fluorescent-lighted, impersonal supermarkets.

Built in 1996, the **New Ag Hall** (35 Panhandle Rd., tel. 508/693–9549), about a mile from the Old Agricultural Hall (☞ above), is the setting for various shows, lectures, dances, and potluck dinners. A yearly county fair—including a woodsman contest, dog show, games, baked goods and jams for sale, and, of course, livestock- and produce-judging—is held here in late August.

A rich and expansive collection of flora and serene walking trails are the attractions of the **Polly Hill Arboretum.** A horticulturist and part-time Vineyard resident, Polly Hill, now in her 90s, has over the years tended some 2,000 species of plants and developed nearly 100 species herself on her old sheep farm in West Tisbury. On site are azaleas, tree peonies, dogwoods, hollies, lilacs, magnolias, and more. Hill raised them from seeds without the use of a greenhouse, and her patience is the inspiration of the arboretum. Now run as a non-profit center, the arboretum also offers guided tours, a lecture series, and a visitor center and gift shop. *809 State Rd., tel. 508/693–9426. $5. Memorial Day–Columbus Day, Thurs.–Tues. 7–7; Columbus Day–Memorial Day, Thurs.–Tues. sunrise–sunset.*

An unusual sight awaits at the **Field Gallery** (State Rd., tel. 508/693–5595), where Tom Maley's ponderous white sculptures, such as a Colonial horse and rider or a whimsical piper, are displayed on a wide lawn. Inside there are changing summer exhibitions of island artists' work, which is for sale.

Music Street, named for the numerous parlor pianos bought with the whaling money of successful sea captains, is lined with the oldest houses in West Tisbury.

NEED A
BREAK?
Step back in time with a visit to **Alley's General Store** (State Rd., tel. 508/693–0088), the heart of town since 1858. Alley's sells a truly general variety of goods: everything from hammers and housewares and dill pickles to all those great things you find only in a country store. There's even a post office inside. The Martha's Vineyard Preservation Trust purchased the building in 1993 and beautified it, preserving its rural character. Behind the parking lot, Back Alley's (tel. 508/693–7367) serves tasty sandwiches and pastries to go year-round.

The **Mill Pond** (Edgartown–West Tisbury Rd.) is a lovely spot graced with swans—at the right time of year you might see a cygnet with the swan couple. The small building nearest the pond has been a grammar school, an icehouse, and most recently a police station, until a larger station house opened.

Martha's Vineyard Trivia

The year-round population of the island is 14,048. On any given day in summer, the population increases seven-fold, to an estimated 102,200.

Some four decades after the island was charted in 1602, Bay Colony businessman Thomas Mayhew struck a deal with the Crown and purchased Martha's Vineyard, as well as Nantucket and the Elizabeth Islands, for £40.

Carly Simon and partners established the island's premier music venue, Hot Tin Roof, in 1979.

Jeanne and Hugh Taylor, the latter the brother of recording star James Taylor, operate the Outermost Inn, by the lighthouse in Aquinnah.

Total shoreline: 126 mi. Total land area: 100 square mi.

Martha's Vineyard was formed more than 20,000 years ago as great sheets of ice, as thick as 2 mi, descended from the frigid northern climes into what is now New England, pushing great chunks of earth and rock before them. When the glaciers melted and receded, the island, as well as Nantucket and Cape Cod, remained in their wake.

When residents say they are going "Up Island," they mean they're heading to the western areas of Aquinnah, Chilmark, Menemsha, and West Tisbury. The designation is based on nautical terminology, where heading west means going "up" in longitude. "Down Island" refers to Vineyard Haven, Oak Bluffs, and Edgartown.

During the height of the 19th-century whaling era, it was considered good luck to have an Aquinnah Wampanoag on board. The Wampanoags were renowned as sailors and harpooners. Town residents voted to change the name of Gay Head to Aquinnah in 1997, and the official change was signed into law on May 7, 1998.

The mill stands across the road. Originally a gristmill, it opened in 1847 to manufacture island wool for pea coats, which whalers wore. The Martha's Vineyard Garden Club uses the building now. The pond is just around the corner from the town center on the way toward Edgartown.

27 Its limbs twisting into the sky and along the ground, the **Old Oak Tree** stands near the intersection of State and North roads. This massive, much-loved member of the *quercus* family is thought to be about 150 years old, and it's a perennial subject for nature photographers.

The **Martha's Vineyard Glassworks** (529 State Rd., N. Tisbury, tel. 508/693–6026) offers a chance to watch glass being blown—a fascinating process—by glassmakers who have pieces displayed in Boston's Museum of Fine Arts. Their work is also for sale.

West Tisbury has a wealth of conservation areas, each of them unique. A paradise for bird-watchers, **Sepiessa Point Reservation,** a Land Bank–Nature Conservancy property, consists of 164 acres on splendid Tisbury Great Pond, with expansive pond and ocean views, walking trails around coves and saltwater marshes, bird-watching, horse trails, swimming, and a boat launch. On the pond beach, watch out for razor-sharp oyster shells. Beaches across the pond along the ocean are privately owned. *New La., which becomes Tiah's Cove Rd., off W. Tisbury Rd., tel. 508/627–7141. Free. Daily sunrise–sunset.*

Long Point, a 633-acre Trustees of Reservations preserve with an open area of grassland and heath, provides a lovely walk with the promise of a refreshing swim at its end. The area is bounded on the east by freshwater Homer's Pond, on the west by saltwater West Tisbury Great Pond, and on the south by fantastic, mile-long South Beach on the Atlantic Ocean. Tisbury Great Pond and Long Cove Pond, a sandy freshwater swimming pond, are ideal spots for bird-watchers. Drinking water and a rest-room facility are available. Arrive early on summer days if

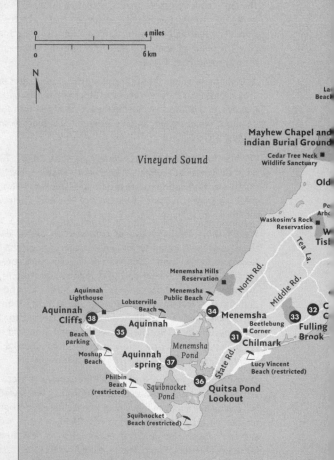

0   4 miles

0   6 km

N

Vineyard Sound

La
Beach

**Mayhew Chapel and
indian Burial Ground**

Cedar Tree Neck ■
Wildlife Sanctuary

Old

Po
Arbo

Waskosim's Rock
Reservation

W
Tisl

Tea La.

North Rd.

Middle Rd.

Menemsha Hills ■
Reservation

Menemsha
Public Beach

Aquinnah
Lighthouse

Lobsterville
Beach

**Aquinnah
Cliffs** **38**

35

Beach
parking ■

Moshup
Beach

Philbin
Beach
(restricted)

Aquinnah

34

Menemsha

Beetlebug ■
Corner

33

32 C
C

Fulling
Brook

31

Chilmark

37

Aquinnah
spring

Menemsha
Pond

Lucy Vincent
Beach (restricted)

Squibnocket
Pond

36

**Quitsa Pond
Lookout**

State Rd.

Squibnocket
Beach (restricted)

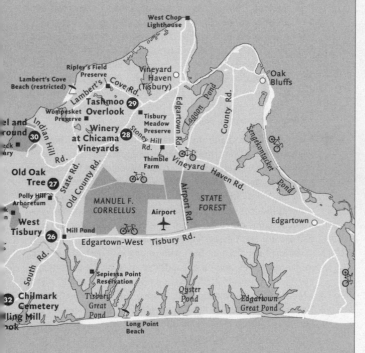

West Chop
Lighthouse ■

Ripley's Field
Preserve ■

Lambert's Cove
Beach (restricted) ■

Lambert's

Cove Rd.

Vineyard
Haven
(Tisbury) ○

Oak
Bluffs ○

Wompesket
Preserve ■

Tashmoo
Overlook **29**

Tisbury
Meadow
Preserve ■

Edgartown Rd.

Lagoon
Pond

County Rd.

Sengekontacket Pond

30

Indian Hill Rd.

Winery
at Chicama
Vineyards **28**

Stoney
Hill
Rd.

Old Oak
Tree **27**

Polly Hill
Arboretum ■

Thimble
Farm ■

Vineyard Haven Rd.

MANUEL F.
CORRELLUS

Airport

✈

STATE
FOREST

Edgartown ○

State Rd.

Old County Rd.

West
Tisbury **26**

Mill Pond ■

Edgartown-West   Tisbury Rd.

South Rd.

Sepiessa Point
Reservation ■

Tisbury
Great
Pond

Oyster
Pond

Edgartown
Great
Pond

32 Chilmark
Cemetery
illing Mill
ook

Long Point
Beach

ATLANTIC OCEAN

you're coming by car, since the lot fills quickly. The **Trustees of Reservations** (tel. 508/693–7392) organizes informative and fun two-hour canoe trips through the reserve. Call ahead to reserve a spot on one of the two trips per day (Friday–Tuesday). *Mid-June–mid-Sept., turn left onto the unmarked dirt road (Waldron's Bottom Rd., look for mailboxes) ³/₁₀ mi west of airport on Edgartown–West Tisbury Rd.; at end, follow signs to Long Point parking lot. Mid-Sept.-mid-June, follow unpaved Deep Bottom Rd. (1 mi west of airport) 2 mi to lot. tel. 508/693–7392. Mid-June–mid-Sept., $7 per vehicle, $3 per adult; free rest of yr. Daily 9–6.*

★ ㉘ A rather unique island undertaking, the **Winery at Chicama Vineyards** is the fruit of the Mathiesen family's labors. From 3 acres of trees and rocks, George—a broadcaster from San Francisco—his wife, Cathy, and their six children have built a fine vineyard. They started in 1971 with 18,000 vinifera vines, and today the winery produces nearly 100,000 bottles a year from chardonnay, cabernet, and other European grapes. Chenin Blanc, merlot, and a cranberry dessert wine are among their 10 or more tasty varieties. A shop selling their wine, along with herbed vinegars, mustards, jellies, and other foods prepared on the premises, is open year-round. A Christmas shop with glassware, gift baskets, wreaths, and wine-related items is open mid-November through New Year's Eve. *Stoney Hill Rd., tel. 508/693–0309. Free tours and tastings. Memorial Day–Columbus Day, Mon.–Sat. 11–5, Sun. 1–5; call for off-season hrs and tastings.*

In season you can pick your own strawberries and raspberries at **Thimble Farm,** where you can also buy preboxed fruit if you're not feeling quite so agrarian. The farm also sells cut flowers, melons, pumpkins, hydroponic tomatoes, and other produce. *Stoney Hill Rd., tel. 508/693–6396. June–early Oct., Tues.–Sun. 10–5.*

㉙ Just outside the center of Vineyard Haven, on the way to West Tisbury, the **Tashmoo Overlook** (State Rd. and Spring St.) surveys a public meadow leading down to Lake Tashmoo and Vineyard Sound beyond. Across the lane from the meadow is the amphitheater where the Vineyard Playhouse holds summer productions.

NEED A BREAK? Part country store and part grocery outlet, **Cronig's Market** (State Rd., tel. 508/693–2234) carries everything from chips and dips to deli supplies and the coolers in which to carry it all to the beach. Cronig's also has another, larger store (State Rd., tel. 508/693–4457) in Vineyard Haven.

One of the rare meadows open for hiking on the island, the 83-acre **Tisbury Meadow Preserve** (trailhead on east side of State Rd., ¼ mi south of Tashmoo Overlook) isn't being farmed but is mowed to keep it from reverting to woodland. An old farmstead sits on the property, and the back acres are wooded except for an 18th-century cart path. You can walk Tisbury Meadow in less than an hour or combine it with two other areas, the Wompesket and Ripley's Fields preserves across State Road, for a longer hike.

Ripley's Field Preserve (John Hoft Rd., off north end of Lambert's Cove Rd., ⅔ mi from State Rd.) gives an idea of what the island must have looked like 200 years ago. The 56-acre preserve spreads over undulating, glacier-formed meadows and woodland. A windmill and wildflowers are pleasant attractions. The preserve connects via old cart paths to Tisbury Meadow and Wompesket preserves in North Tisbury. A parking area and bike rack are on the left.

Bordering part of Merry Farm, **Wompesket Preserve** (Red Coat Hill Rd.) includes an interesting wet meadow and ponds that are good for birding. The walk to the 18-acre area overlooks the farm and the Atlantic in the distance. To get here, follow marked dirt roads from Ripley's Field or Tisbury Meadow Preserve.

30 Deep in the woods off a dirt road, the **Mayhew Chapel and Indian Burial Ground** (off Indian Hill Rd., off State Rd.) are suffused with history. The tiny chapel, built in 1829 to replace an earlier one, and a memorial plaque are dedicated to the pastor Thomas Mayhew, Jr., leader of the original colonists who landed at Edgartown in 1642. Mayhew was noted for his fair dealings with the local Wampanoags. Within a few years, he had converted a number of them to Christianity. Called Praying Indians, they established a community here called Christiantown.

An overgrown wildflower garden grows near the chapel. Beyond the boulder with the plaque are rough-hewn stones marking Native American grave mounds—the dead are not named, for fear of calling down evil spirits. Behind the chapel is the beginning of the Christiantown Woods loop trail, which leads to a lookout tower. You'll find a map at the head of the trail.

Cedar Tree Neck Wildlife Sanctuary, 250 hilly acres of unspoiled West Tisbury woods managed by the Sheriff's Meadow Foundation, consists of varied environments, among them a sphagnum bog and a pond. The sanctuary has interesting flora, including bayberry and swamp azalea bushes, tupelo, sassafras, and pygmy beech trees. Wooded trails lead to a stony but secluded North Shore beach (swimming, picnicking, and fishing prohibited), and from the summit of a headland there are views of Aquinnah and the Elizabeth Islands. To get here, follow Indian Hill Road off State Road for 2 mi, and then turn right 1 mi on Obed Daggett Road, an occasionally steep, rocky dirt road to the parking lot. *Indian Hill Rd., tel. 508/693–5207. Free. Daily 8:30–5:30.*

★ At the center of the island, the **Manuel F. Correllus State Forest** is a 5,000-acre pine and scrub-oak forest crisscrossed with hiking trails and circled by a paved but rough bike trail (mopeds are prohibited). There's a 2-mi nature trail, a 2-mi par fitness course, and horse trails. The West Tisbury side of the state forest joins with an equally large Edgartown parcel to virtually surround the airport. *Headquarters on Barnes Rd. by the airport, tel. 508/693–2540. Free. Daily sunrise–sunset.*

A memorial to Thomas Mayhew, Jr., called **Place on the Wayside,** stands along Edgartown–West Tisbury Road, just east of the airport entrance on the south side of the road. A plaque identifies the spot where Mayhew had his "last worship and interview with them [the Wampanoags] before embarking for England" in 1657, never to return: the ship was lost at sea. Wampanoags passing this spot would leave a stone in Mayhew's memory, and the stones were later cemented together to form the memorial.

CHILMARK

31 5½ mi southwest of West Tisbury, 12 mi southwest of Vineyard Haven

A rural, unspoiled village with scenic ocean-view roads, rustic woodlands, and no crowds, Chilmark draws chic summer visitors and, hard on their heels, stratospheric real-estate prices. Lucy Vincent Beach (residents only in summer) here is perhaps the island's most beautiful. Laced with ribbons of rough roads and winding stone fences that once separated fields and pastures, Chilmark reminds visitors what the Vineyard was like in an earlier time, before developers took over.

Waskosim's Rock Reservation, bought by the Land Bank in 1990 from a developer who had planned to build 40 houses on it, comprises diverse habitats—rolling green hills, wetlands, oak and black gum woods, and 1,500 ft of frontage on Mill Brook—as well as the ruins of an 18th-century homestead. Waskosim's Rock itself was deposited by the retreating glacier 10,000 years ago and is said to resemble the head of a breaching whale. It is one of the highest points on the Vineyard, situated on a ridge above the valley, from which there is a panoramic view of more than 1,000 acres of protected land. At the trailhead off North Road, a map outlines a 3-mi hike throughout the 166 acres. Parking areas on North Rd., tel. 508/627–7141. Free. Daily sunrise–sunset.

32 ABEL'S HILL CEMETERY (South Rd.) offers an interesting look into the island's past. Longtime summer resident and writer Lillian Hellman, one of many who continued the Vineyard's tradition of liberal politics, is buried here, as is John Belushi, in an unmarked grave. A boulder, engraved with the comedian's name, sits near the entrance. A few steps away is a headstone sporting a skull and crossbones, with the notation "Here Lies the Body of John Belushi. I May Be Gone but Rock and Roll Lives On"; common knowledge is that it's a decoy placed to deter overzealous fans from finding the actual burial site. Visitors often leave, as tokens of remembrance, empty champagne bottles, cigarette butts, flowers, and notes.

Beetlebung Corner (Middle, State, South, and Menemsha Cross Rds.), a crossroads named for the tupelo, or black gum, trees that grow here, which were used to make wooden mallets and plugs for casks (called "beetles" and "bungs"), marks Chilmark's town center. Here are the town's public buildings, including the firehouse and the post office, as well as the **Chilmark Community Center** (tel. 508/645–9484), where events such as town meetings, auctions, children's activities, and chamber music concerts take place. In summer, a general store, a clothing boutique, a restaurant and breakfast café, a gallery, and a bank turn the little crossroads into a mini-metropolis.

NEED A BREAK? The **Chilmark Store** (7 State Rd., tel. 508/645–3655) has the basics that you'd expect as well as Primo's Pizza, a solid take-out lunch spot. If you've bicycled into town, the wooden rockers on the porch may be just the place to take a break—or find a picnic spot of your own nearby to enjoy a fish burger or a slice of the pizza of the day. It's open from May to mid-October.

33 Jointly owned by the Land Bank and the town, **Fulling Mill Brook** (Middle or South Rd.) is a 50-acre conservation area. Its easy walking trail slopes gently down toward the lowlands along the brook, where there are boulders to sit and sun on, and to the property's edge at South Road, where there's a bike rack.

MENEMSHA

★ (34) *1½ mi northwest of Chilmark, 3½ mi east of Aquinnah.*

A fishing village unspoiled by the "progress" of the past few decades, Menemsha is a jumble of weathered fishing shacks, fishing and pleasure boats, drying nets and lobster pots, and parents and kids pole-fishing from the jetty. Though the picturesque scene is not lost on myriad photographers and artists, this is very much a working village. The catch of the day, taken off boats returning to port, is sold at markets along Dutcher's Dock. Romantics bring picnic suppers to the public **Menemsha Beach** to catch perfect sunsets over the water. If you feel you've seen this town before, you probably have: it was used for location shots in the film *Jaws*.

Very different from most other island conservation areas, **Menemsha Hills Reservation,** a 210-acre Trustees of Reservations property, includes a mile of rocky shoreline and high sand bluffs along Vineyard Sound. Its hilly walking trails through scrub oak and heathland have interpretive signs at viewing points, and the 309-ft Prospect Hill, the island's highest, affords excellent views of the Elizabeth Islands and beyond. Call ahead about naturalist-led tours. *Off North Rd., 1 mi east of Menemsha Cross Rd., tel. 508/693–7662. Free. Daily sunrise–sunset.*

AQUINNAH

(35) *4 mi west of Menemsha, 12 mi southwest of West Tisbury, 20 mi west of Edgartown.*

Aquinnah, formerly called Gay Head, is an official Native American township. In 1987, after more than a decade of struggle in the courts, the Wampanoag tribe won guardianship of 420 acres of land, which are held in trust by the federal government in perpetuity and constitute the Aquinnah Native American Reservation. In 1997, the town voted to change the town's name from Gay Head back to its original Native American name, Aquinnah (pronounced a-kwih-nah), Wampanoag for "Land Under the Hill." While the name has changed, it will take some time for the state and Martha's Vineyard authorities to convert road signs, maps, and other documents to the new name—so you can expect minor confusion. Some private businesses that use the name Gay Head might elect to retain it, so keep in mind that Gay Head and Aquinnah refer to the same place.

The "center" of Aquinnah consists of a combination fire and police station, the town hall, a Tribal Council office, and a public library, formerly the little red schoolhouse. Because the town's year-round population hovers around 650, Aquinnah children attend schools in other towns.

36 **QUITSA POND LOOKOUT** (State Rd.) has a good view of the adjoining Menemsha and Nashaquitsa ponds, the woods, and the ocean beyond.

37 **AQUINNAH SPRING** (State Rd.) is channeled through a roadside iron pipe, gushing water cold enough to slake a cyclist's thirst on the hottest day. Feel free to fill a canteen. Locals come from all over the island to fill jugs. The spring is on the left, clearly visible from the road, a tenth of a mile past the Aquinnah town line sign.

★ **38** The spectacular, dramatically striated walls of red clay at **Aquinnah Cliffs** (State Rd.), a National Historic Landmark and part of the Wampanoag reservation land, are the island's major tourist attraction, as evidenced by the tour bus–filled parking lot. Native American crafts and food shops line the short approach to the overlook, from which you can see the Elizabeth Islands to the northeast across Vineyard Sound and Noman's Land Island, part wildlife preserve, part military bombing-practice site, 3 mi off the Vineyard's southern coast.

If you've reached a state of quiet, vacation-land bliss, keep in mind that this is a heavily touristed spot, and it might turn out to be a shock to your peace of mind. When you come, consider going to Aquinnah Lighthouse (☞ *below*) first, then down and around to the beach and cliffs. If you're famished when you arrive, you can eat at L'Osteria at the Aquinnah (☞ Chapter 3), at the top of the loop by the lighthouse.

There is no immediate access to the beach from the light—nothing like an easy staircase down the cliffs to the sand below. To reach the cliffs, park in the Moshup Beach (☞ Beaches in Outdoor Activities and Sports, *below*) lot by the lighthouse loop, walk five-plus minutes south on the boardwalk, then continue another 20 or more minutes on the sand to get back around to the lighthouse. The cliffs themselves are pretty marvelous, and you should plan ahead if you want to see them. It takes a while to get to Aquinnah from elsewhere on the island, and in summer the parking lot and beach fill up, so start early to get a jump on the throngs.

Aquinnah Lighthouse, adjacent to the Aquinnah Cliffs overlook, is the largest of the Vineyard's five, precariously stationed atop the rapidly eroding cliffs. In 1799 a wooden lighthouse was built here—the island's first—to warn ships of Devil's Bridge, an area of shoals ¼ mi offshore. The current incarnation, built in 1856 of red brick, carries on with its alternating pattern of red and white flashes. Despite the light, the Vineyard's worst wreck occurred here in January 1884, when the *City of Columbus* sank, taking with it into the icy waters more than 100 passengers and crew. The original Fresnel lens was removed when the lighthouse was automated in 1952, and it is preserved at the Vineyard Museum in Edgartown (☞ *above*). The lighthouse is open to the public for sunsets Friday, Saturday, and Sunday in summer, weather permitting; private tours can also be arranged. *Lighthouse Rd., tel.* 508/645–2211. $2.

Your checklist for a perfect journey

WAY AHEAD

- Devise a trip budget.
- Write down the five things you want most from this trip. Keep this list handy before and during your trip.
- Make plane or train reservations. Book lodging and rental cars.
- Arrange for pet care.
- Check your passport. Apply for a new one if necessary.
- Photocopy important documents and store in a safe place.

A MONTH BEFORE

- Make restaurant reservations and buy theater and concert tickets. Visit fodors.com for links to local events.
- Familiarize yourself with the local language or lingo.

TWO WEEKS BEFORE

- Replenish your supply of medications.
- Create your itinerary.
- Enjoy a book or movie set in your destination to get you in the mood.

- Develop a packing list. Shop for missing essentials. Repair and launder or dry-clean your clothes.

A WEEK BEFORE

- Stop newspaper deliveries. Pay bills.
- Acquire traveler's checks.
- Stock up on film.
- Label your luggage.
- Finalize your packing list— take less than you think you need.
- Create a toiletries kit filled with travel-size essentials.
- Get lots of sleep. Don't get sick before your trip.

A DAY BEFORE

- Drink plenty of water.
- Check your travel documents.
- Get packing!

DURING YOUR TRIP

- Keep a journal/scrapbook.
- Spend time with locals.
- Take time to explore. Don't plan too much.

A scenic route worth the trip is West Basin Road, which takes you along the Vineyard Sound shore of Menemsha Light and through the **Cranberry Lands,** an area of cranberry bogs gone wild that is a popular nesting site for birds. No humans can nest here, but you can drive by and look. At the end of the road, with marshland on the right and low dunes, grasses, and the long blue arc of the bight on the left, you get a terrific view of the quiet fishing village of Menemsha, across the water. **Lobsterville Road Beach** here is public, but public parking is limited to three spots, so get here early if you want one of them.

Three young women sit huddled around a table at the Navigator. "What's going on here?" they ask each other. They're frequent visitors to Martha's Vineyard and each time they've been here before they've had a fabulous time. In the bars and bistros of Circuit Avenue in Oak Bluffs, on Main Street and beyond in Edgartown, the Island has always been teeming with guys scouting out fun, romance, or relationships. But now, on this balmy night in September, even though there are more men in the bars than they've ever seen before, the young women just can't seem to attract any attention. The men lean against the bar, intently checking newpapers, gesturing lengths with their hands, and welcome each new male that arrives. As a waiter passes their table, the bravest of the three women catches his arm. "Excuse me," she ventures. "Is there something going on around here that we don't know about? "The waiter looks puzzled at first, then recognition dawns on his face. "Oh, boy, have you come at the wrong time," he explains. "The only way you're going to get any attention is if you're wearing bluefish cologne. It's the fishing derby!"

In This Chapter

By Joyce Wagner

nightlife and the arts

MAYBE YOU'VE COME TO MARTHA'S VINEYARD looking for a a great night out on the town; or perhaps you want to immerse yourself in the local culture; or maybe this vacation you want to explore your creative urges. No matter what it is you seek, you've come to the right place—the Vineyard has all this and more. During the summer, clubs, concerts, plays, gallery openings, dances, and classes in art, music, dance, and writing abound. A bonus for families is that many activities take place without the presence of alcohol: it may seem impossible in these modern times, but most of the Vineyard is dry. In fact, liquor licenses are issued only in Edgartown and Oak Bluffs. It's in these two towns that you'll find the bulk of clubs and entertainment venues.

Since the year-round atmosphere on the island is nurturing to artists of all kinds, the home-grown talent here is phenomenal. Sponsors such as Featherstone Meetinghouse for the Arts and Rising Tide produce concerts of mostly local talent, and you'll find many local and off-island performing artists entertaining at your favorite bistro. Classical, folk, pop, and other musical concerts can be seen at the Old Whaling Church in Edgartown, at the Tabernacle in Oak Bluffs, and at the Chilmark Community Center. The Hot Tin Roof provides more lively fare, including jazz, salsa, and rock. If you're looking to indulge in a new hobby, improve on an old one, or just get in touch with your inner artist, classes are available in fine art, dancing, photography, writing, and even healthy cooking at places like Featherstone Meetinghouse for the Arts, the Yard, Nathan Mayhew Seminars, and the Martha's Vineyard Wellness Center.

How and Where

In Edgartown and Oak Bluffs—the two wet towns on the island—restaurants that serve lunch, and their attached bars, usually open at around 11 AM, Monday through Saturday, and at noon on Sunday. Restaurants that serve dinner only open around 5:30 or 6. Last call is around 12:30 for a 1 AM closing. Most credit cards are accepted. Although the dress code is almost always casual at island nightspots, beachwear is welcome at none. Bring a sweater, even in the summer, if you're going to be anywhere near the water.

During the summer, expect to wait in line at the more popular venues. A word of warning for underage drinkers: all of the island's bars check IDs. Many of the door personnel are police officers by day and are well-trained to spot falsified identification. If you try to sneak in you may not be just turned away—you could be arrested.

Sources

Both **island newspapers,** the *Martha's Vineyard Times* and the *Vineyard Gazette*, as well as the *Cape Cod Times*, publish weekly calendars of events. Also scan the *Best Read Guide*, free at many shops and hotels.

The 24-hour movie hot line (tel. 508/627–6689) has schedules for the **Capawock** (Main St., Vineyard Haven), **Island Theater** (Circuit Ave., Oak Bluffs), and the **Strand** (Oak Bluffs Ave. Ext., Oak Bluffs). **Entertainment Cinemas** (Main St., Edgartown, tel. 508/627–8008) has two screens showing first-release films. Films are also shown at other locations from time to time, so check local papers.

DOWN-ISLAND

VINEYARD HAVEN (TISBURY)

Island Theatre Workshop (tel. 508/693–5290) is the island's oldest year-round company. Under the direction of Lee Fierro, the group performs at various venues and has a summer theater arts program for children.

At **Nathan Mayhew Seminars** (N. William St., tel. 508/696–8428) you'll learn to master the mambo, rhumba, waltz, fox-trot, and cha-cha. Basic steps are taught at 7:30 PM and dancing continues till 9:30 PM. A donation of $3 is requested.

The **Vineyard Playhouse** (24 Church St., tel. 508/693–6450 or 508/696–6300) has a year-round schedule of community theater and professional productions. Mid-June through early September, a mostly Equity troupe performs drama, classics, and comedies on the air-conditioned main stage, as well as summer Shakespeare and other productions at the natural amphitheater at Tashmoo Overlook on State Road in Vineyard Haven—bring insect repellent and a blanket or lawn chair. Children's programs and a summer camp are also offered, as well as local art exhibitions throughout the year. One performance of each summer main-stage show is interpreted in American sign language. The theater is fully handicapped accessible and offers hearing-aid devices.

The **Vineyard Haven Town Band** (tel. 508/645–3458) is the oldest continuing performing arts band on the island. Hear the group in concert at 8 PM every Sunday during the summer, alternating between Owen Park in Vineyard Haven and at the gazebo in Ocean Park on Beach Road in Oak Bluffs. Bring a blanket or beach chair and a picnic if you'd like. The concerts are free.

OAK BLUFFS
Arts

At the **Featherstone Meetinghouse for the Arts** (Barnes Rd., tel. 508/693–1850), classes are available in photography, watercolor, pottery, woodworking, screen printing, drawing, stained glass, weaving, music, and more. During the summer, there's a 6:30 to 8 PM Musical Mondays program with off- and on-island talent performing on the lawn. Admission is $5, free for well-behaved kids; bring a blanket or lawn chair.

Martha's Vineyard Center for the Visual Arts (at the Firehouse Gallery on Dukes County and Vineyard Aves., tel. 508/693–3651) holds art classes throughout the summer. Watch the local papers or call for a schedule.

The **Tabernacle** (Trinity Park at the Methodist Camp Grounds behind Circuit Ave.) is the scene of a popular, old-fashioned-style, Wednesday-evening community sing-along at 8 PM, as well as other family-oriented entertainment. For a schedule, contact the **Camp Meeting Association** (Box 1176, Oak Bluffs 02557, tel. 508/693–0525).

Union Chapel (Kennebec Ave., tel. 508/696–8946) presents Wondrous Wednesdays, organ and piano recitals at noon during the summer, as well as other musical events such as the popular Constant Family String Trio.

Sunday-night summer **Vineyard Haven Town Band concerts** (tel. 508/645–3458) (☞ Vineyard Haven, *above*) alternate weekly locations between the gazebo in Ocean Park on Beach Road in Oak Bluffs and Owen Park in Vineyard Haven. Admission is free.

Nightlife

Atlantic Connection (19 Circuit Ave., tel. 508/693–7129) offers fancy light and sound systems (including a strobe-lighted dance floor topped by a glitter ball) to highlight live reggae, R&B, funk, blues, and disco on weeknights and DJ dancing on Friday and Saturday nights. Watch for island band favorites Entrain and also the Boogies. Monday night is Teen Night for ages 14 to 19 with an admission charge of $10 and free non-alcoholic beverages.

At the far end of Circuit Ave., **Bar None** (57 Circuit Ave., at Balance Restaurant, tel. 508/696–3000) is the only club on the island with a pub food menu that is served till midnight. The lighting is nice, the music's not too loud, and the service is friendly. Although the food and drinks are a little pricey, it's a nice getaway from the craziness of the Oak Bluffs weekend bar scene.

Push through the swinging doors at the **Island House** (11 Circuit Ave., tel. 508/693–4516) and you'll find yourself in a large, dark, crowded, friendly, and smoky bar.

The **Lampost** (6 Circuit Ave., tel. 508/696–9352) is a good, old-fashioned neighborhood bar with a DJ and dancing. In addition to events such as an '80s night, a Brazilian night, and a Hawaiian night, there are also swing and salsa nights where the appropriate dance steps are taught. The bar is popular with a young crowd.

Lola's (Beach Rd., tel. 508/693–5007), a popular restaurant (☞ Chapter 3), has a lively bar that features live jazz and a great pub menu year-round. You can also get regular restaurant cuisine at the bar.

Nancy's (29 Lake Ave., on the harbor, tel. 508/693–0006) is basically a beer and wine bar, but it is fully licensed for mixed drinks. The entire bar is open to the harbor with tables outside and sheltered, and it's a popular spot for boaters. There is also a full menu that includes seafood, sandwiches, and Middle Eastern cuisine.

The island's only brewpub, **Offshore Ale** (Kennebec Ave., tel. 508/693–2626), has live entertainment (usually jazz) year-round, as well as its own great beer and ales and a terrific pub menu. A **beer school** is held year-round on alternate Thursdays at 7 PM by brewmaster Michael Andrews. You'll learn about the

Possible Dreams and Celeb Sightings

The unofficial rule regarding celebrities on Martha's Vineyard is "look, but don't touch." While most of them appreciate a smile or a nod of recognition, the majority don't like to be disturbed while on vacation. If you promise to leave them alone while they're eating, shopping, or sunbathing, we'll tell you where to see the whole lot of them at once: the annual Possible Dreams auction.

Held on the first Monday in August on the lawn of the Harborside Inn in Edgartown, the event is traditionally hosted by Art Buchwald and is attended by celebrity auctioneers, donors, and audience members. You might see Mike Wallace, who usually occupies a seat in the first row, holding court with Katharine Graham. Carly Simon is a regular both in the audience and on the dais. Other celebrities who have made appearances include Merv Griffin, Mike Nichols, Walter Cronkite, William Styron, and the fabulous Patricia Neal. The real stars at the Possible Dreams auction are the items up for bid. Past lots have included two Carly Simon concerts in the high-bidders' homes, which garnered bids of $80,000 each; a bike ride with the late John F. Kennedy, Jr. ($12,500); lunch and tennis with Mike Nichols and Diane Sawyer ($30,000); and a private walk on the beach with James Taylor ($12,500). Other high-ticket items have included walk-on parts in film and television, attendance (with limo service, natch) to the Oscars and Emmys, and a bagel-baking session with Ted Danson and Mary Steenburgen.

If these prices are a little steep for your pocketbook, lower-priced items such as artwork and boat charters are also available for bidding. The proceeds benefit island charities through Martha's Vineyard Community Services. The auction begins at 5, cocktails and other refreshments are available, and admission is $20—worth every penny if you're a celeb watcher. Check local papers for ticket outlets.

evolution, history, and processing of ales, stouts, and other brews and then get a taste of what you've been talking about. The class is limited to 10, so be sure to call ahead to reserve a spot.

The **Rare Duck** (6 Circuit Ave., tel. 508/696–9352), next to the Lampost, is a dark cocktail lounge with live rock, blues, and acoustic music.

The **Ritz Café** (4 Circuit Ave., tel. 508/693–9851) is a popular year-round bar with a jukebox and a pool table that's removed in the summer to make way for dancing. There's an eclectic mix of live performances including hip-hop, blues, and reggae, Monday through Saturday in summer and on weekends in the off-season.

Season's Eatery (19 Circuit Ave., tel. 508/693–7129) shares an owner and management with its next-door neighbor, the Atlantic Connection. There's live acoustic music year-round as well as karaoke on Tuesday and Thursday nights.

Enjoy the harbor view at **Tsunami** (6 Circuit Ave. Ext., tel. 508/693–2453) while you sip on a fabulous sake martini—a blend of passionfruit juice, sake, and plum wine. The bar boasts friendly, professional bartenders and DJ'd house music.

EDGARTOWN
Arts

Old Sculpin Gallery (Dock St., tel. 508/627–4881) holds classes such as watercolor and life drawing for adults and various art classes for children throughout the summer. Call for a schedule.

The **Old Whaling Church** (89 Main St., tel. 508/627–4442) boasts a schedule of classical, pop, and other musical events in the summer and community activities in the off-season, in a beautiful, acoustically grand old church. Watch the papers, or check the kiosk out front for a listing of events.

Nightlife

The downstairs bar at **Alchemy** (71 Main St., tel. 508/627–9999) is fun and friendly and the restaurant's excellent fare is available, too. Food and drink are a bit pricey but worth it. The upstairs bar is small, loud, smoky, and crowded and you have to go through the restaurant to reach it; however, it does have a pool table to entertain the crowd of thirty- and fortysomethings.

The **Atria Bar** (137 Main St., tel. 508/627–5850) is off the beaten path but is a quiet, comfortable place to escape the summer crowds. Enjoy one of the clever martinis, including the "Mochatini" (Stolichnaya Vanil vodka, Godiva Dark Chocolate Liqueur, Kahlua, and Frangelico) and the "Espresso Martini" (Ketel One vodka, Kahlua, Tia Maria, and a shot of fresh espresso). You'll also find microbrew beer and an extensive wine. Play a game of bumper pool, curl up on one of the leather sofas, or sit at the bar and watch the tropical fish.

The **Boathouse Bar** (2 Main St., tel. 508/627–4320) is the closest thing Edgartown has to a singles scene. Right on the harbor, it attracts mostly boat enthusiasts of all ages and is a large, noisy party bar with dancing and rock bands. If the noise becomes too much, you can take your drink out on the patio and watch the boats sail in and out of the harbor.

The **Carlos Fuentes Cigar Bar** (131 N. Water St., in the Harbor View Hotel, tel. 508/627–3761) is a small, smoky bar that dispenses high-end liquors, fine cigars, and a gorgeous view of the Edgartown lighthouse. The ambience is good old boys' club, with lots of dark wood in the decor. When the smoke overwhelms you, there's a porch where you can enjoy your drink and the view.

David Ryan's Restaurant and Cafe (11 N. Water St., tel. 508/ 627–4100) is packed with an older, lively crowd in summer and is a hang-out for locals in the winter. It's crowded and smoky and there's no music, but people seem to like it. You may have to wait in line to squeeze in.

Hideaway Pub (44 N. Water, tel. 508/627–6655) is aptly named for its location behind the Shiretown Inn and for the intimacy of its bar. There are two sections, one with tables and the other with couches. Food from the Shiretown restaurant is available in either section. Share an appetizer with someone special and cuddle to the cool live jazz of Anna Cole and her quintet.

Hot Tin Roof (Martha's Vineyard Airport, Edgartown–West Tisbury Rd., tel. 508/693–1137), opened by Carly Simon in 1976, is a venue for big-name acts such as Jimmy Cliff, Jerry Lee Lewis, Kate Taylor, Andreas Vollenweider, and King Creole and the Coconuts. Dance to reggae, salsa, rock, and jazz, surrounded by fanciful murals by Margot Datz. When you're ready for a break, there's a raw bar on the patio.

The **Newes from America** (Kelley House, Kelly St., tel. 508/627–4397) is quieter than most of the island's pubs, and the exposed wooden beams, fireplace, and brick walls of the circa 1742 building create a cozy ambience. Order one of the 13 microbrewery beers on tap or a snack from the bar menu. You'll probably notice the piles of wooden nickels in front of bar patrons: you get one wooden nickel for each short draught and two nickels for each tall draught you order. Collect 500 and you earn yourself a spot on the Declaration of Distinction and a personalized ½-yard glass, which becomes yours to drink from at subsequent visits (they hold on to it for you).

The **Wharf Pub** (Lower Main St., tel. 508/627–9966) is stuffed with young, friendly party people in the summer and crusty fishermen in the winter.

UP-ISLAND

WEST TISBURY

M.V. Wellness Center (489 State Rd., tel. 508/696–0644) holds classes year-round in dance, yoga, and healthy cooking. Call for a schedule.

West Tisbury Library (State Rd. at West Tisbury Center, tel. 508/693–3366) shows vintage, classic, and children's movies every Monday night, year-round (with more family fare in the summer), at 7. Check the local papers or call for a schedule.

WIMP (Grange Hall, State Rd., tel. 508/696–8475) is the island's not-to-be-missed premier comedy improvisation troupe. The group performs Wednesday night at 8 PM from mid-June to mid-October.

CHILMARK

The **Chilmark Community Center** (Beetlebung Corner, tel. 508/645–9484) holds square dances, concerts, and other events for families throughout the summer. Watch for announcements in the papers.

Find the writer in you at **Chilmark Writing Workshop** (tel. 508/645–9085), a series of four morning classes held weekly during the summer. Lead by Nancy Slonim Aronie—a teaching fellow at Harvard University, author of "Writing from the Heart," and a former NPR commentator—the workshop is held in the sculpture garden of her Chilmark home (or in her living room if it rains) and provides a safe and nurturing atmosphere for self-expression. This is a very popular course for year-round islanders as well as visitors. It's best to reserve a spot in the spring for summer classes.

Martha's Vineyard Chamber Music Society (tel. 508/696–8055), formerly called the Chilmark Chamber Players, performs 10 summer concerts and 3 in winter at various venues.

WIMP: Big Laughs on a Small Island

The very thought of "audience participation" sounds as enticing as walking on glass for many people, but WIMP, the island's comedy improvisation troupe, will put you at ease while providing laughs-a-plenty. Fear not: You'll never be dragged onto the stage and embarrassed. The extent of your participation is to call out ideas that the troupe then incorporates into theater games. The result is comedy that's always fresh and never scripted. Founded by local actors in 1993, the group performed weekly at the now defunct Wintertide Coffee House (from which it attained its name, short for Wintertide Improv), and has recently found a new arena at the Grange Hall in West Tisbury. This group is tight. Every one of the eight members has his or her own comedy groove, but their ensemble work is so refined, you can almost see ideas bouncing silently between them. The subject matter is suitable for older children (PG-13) and adults; and, as if making the Vineyard safe for laughter is not enough, the group donates all of its profits to island charities.

The **Yard** (off Middle Rd., tel. 508/645-9662)—a colony of dancers and choreographers formed in 1973—gives several performances throughout the summer at its 100-seat barn theater in a wooded setting. Artists are selected each year from auditions held in New York. Dance classes are available to visitors.

If ghosts indeed exist, the old inn is the type of place where they ought to be, and are rumored to be. The downstairs tavern is dark, with 300-year-old, hand hewn ceiling beams, creaky wood floors, and a massive hearth, the type that used to heat an entire room. The sense, both comforting and startling, is that many a road-weary boot has trod these floors. The barman has seen this look before. "The rooms here are lovely," he says, "maybe a few bumps in the night, but you'll sleep like a baby."

In This Chapter

Updated by Karl Luntta

where to stay

THE VARIETY OF LODGING on Martha's Vineyard ranges from historic whaling captains' mansions filled with antiques to sprawling modern oceanfront hotels to cozy cottages in the woods. When choosing your accommodations, keep in mind that each town has a different "personality": Oak Bluffs tends to cater to a younger, active, nightlife-oriented crowd, while Edgartown is more subdued. Chilmark has beautiful beaches and miles of conservation lands but not much of a downtown shopping area. Bear in mind that many of the island's B&Bs, set in vintage homes filled with art and antiques, have age restrictions—call ahead if you're traveling with a family. And remember that in July and August, the height of the summer season, minimum stays of as many as three nights may be required. If you're planning to visit for a week or more, you might consider renting a house.

Prices

Advance reservations for summer stays should be made as far in advance as possible; early spring is not too early. Rates in season are very high but may go down by as much as 50% in the off-season. All rooms described below have private bath, unless otherwise noted.

CATEGORY	COST*
$$$$	over $200
$$$	$150–$200
$$	$100–$150
$	under $100

*for a standard double room in high season, excluding gratuities and

*a 5.7% state tax plus an additional 4% room tax levied locally.
Some inns add a 15% service charge.*

DOWN-ISLAND

VINEYARD HAVEN (TISBURY)

$$$$ THORNCROFT INN. Set on 3½ wooded acres about 1 mi from the ferry, this inn's main building, a 1918 Craftsman bungalow, combines fine Colonial and richly carved Renaissance Revival antiques with tasteful reproductions to create a somewhat formal environment. Ten of the rooms have working fireplaces. Deluxe rooms are outfitted with minirefrigerators, and some have canopy beds; three rooms have two-person whirlpool baths and two have private hot-tub spas. Set apart from the main house and reached via a breezeway, the private, ultradeluxe room has a king-size bed and a whirlpool tub and is wheelchair accessible. Owners Karl and Lynn Buder deliver a newspaper to your room each morning and serve full breakfasts in two seatings (or breakfast in bed), as well as afternoon tea. No smoking is permitted. *460 Main St., Box 1022, 02568, tel. 508/693–3333 or 800/332–1236, fax 508/693–5419. 14 rooms. Library. AE, D, DC, MC, V. BP. www.thorncroft.com*

$$$–$$$$ HANOVER HOUSE. Set on ½ acre of landscaped lawn within walking distance of the ferry, this inn offers comfortable rooms decorated with a combination of antiques and reproduction furniture. Each room has its individual flair, some with floral wallpaper and quilts, others sponge-painted and filled with whimsical, creative furnishings such as an antique sewing machine that serves as a TV stand. Three suites in the separate carriage house are roomy, with private decks or patios; two have kitchenettes. Owners Tom Richardson and Teri Cook include touches such as Hemingway paperbacks on night tables. Homemade breads and muffins and a special house cereal are served each morning on a sunporch brightened with fresh flowers from the gardens. There are no phones in the rooms; however, guests can use the house computer to access their e-mail. *28 Edgartown Rd., Box 2107, 02568, tel. 508/693–1066 or 800/339–1066, fax 508/696–6099. 11 rooms, 3 suites. No pets, no smoking. Air-conditioning. AE, D, MC, V. Closed Dec.– Mar. CP. www.hanoverhouseinn.com*

\$\$\$–\$\$\$\$ **MARTHA'S PLACE.** Since it opened in 1997, Martin Hicks and
★ Richard Alcott's B&B has set a standard on the island. This 1840s Greek Revival house, built by a descendant of the island's founder, bubbles with hospitality. The interior's carefully selected antiques and luscious fabrics reveal the presence of a design pro (Martin); he never spills over into frou-frou. Then there are the generous details: thick terry-cloth robes, beautifully presented Continental breakfasts, and tennis rackets and bicycles provided gratis to guests. The property overlooks the harbor (some rooms have water views); it's a few blocks from the ferry landing, just west of the village center. *114 Main St., Box 1182, 02568, tel./fax 508/693–0253. 6 rooms. Breakfast room, bicycles. AE, MC, V. CP. www.marthasplace.com*

\$\$–\$\$\$\$ **CAPTAIN DEXTER HOUSE.** An 1843 sea captain's house at the edge of the shopping district is the setting for this intimate B&B. Small guest rooms are appointed with period-style wallpapers, velvet wing chairs, and 18th-century antiques and reproductions, including several four-poster canopy beds with lace or fishnet canopies and hand-sewn quilts. The Captain Harding Room is larger, with the original wood floor as well as a fireplace, bay windows, canopy bed, desk, and bright bath with claw-foot tub. There is a common refrigerator, and in season, afternoon lemonade and cookies and evening sherry are served. *92 Main St., Box 2457, 02568, tel. 508/693–6564, fax 508/693–8448. 7 rooms, 1 suite. Air-conditioning. No pets, no smoking. AE, MC, V. CP.*

\$\$–\$\$\$\$ **CROCKER HOUSE INN.** This 1924 farmhouse-style inn is tucked into a quiet side street off Main Street, minutes from the ferries and Owen Park Beach. The eight bright rooms are decorated in woods

vineyard haven lodging

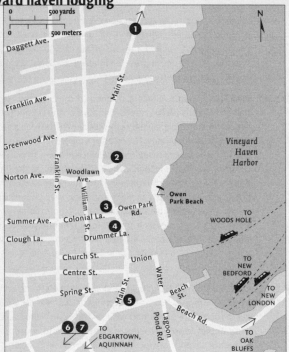

0 ____ 500 yards
0 ____ 500 meters

Daggett Ave.

Main St.

Franklin Ave.

Greenwood Ave.

Franklin St.

Norton Ave.

Woodlawn Ave.

William St.

Summer Ave.

Colonial La.

Clough La.

Drummer La.

Church St.

Centre St.

Spring St.

Main St.

Union

Water St.

Beach St.

Lagoon Pond Rd.

Beach Rd.

Owen Park Rd.

Owen Park Beach

Vineyard Haven Harbor

N

TO WOODS HOLE

TO NEW BEDFORD

TO NEW LONDON

TO OAK BLUFFS

TO EDGARTOWN, AQUINNAH

❶ ❷ ❸ ❹ ❺ ❻ ❼

Captain Dexter House, 4

Crocker House Inn, 2

Hanover House, 6

Martha's Place, 3

Martha's Vineyard Family Campground, 7

Thorncroft Inn, 1

Tisbury Inn, 5

and country decor and have private baths, telephones, and TVs (on request). Mounted on the wall is a small "honor bar," with such items as disposable camera, sun lotion, and more. Three rooms come with soothing whirlpool hot tubs, and two have fireplaces. No. 6, with a small porch and a private entrance, has the best view of the harbor, but the most popular room is the third-floor loft (No. 8), set amid the odd angles of the roof. The room has plenty of sleeping space, including a pullout couch, as well as a gas stove and a two-person hot tub. Breakfast is served at a large farmer's table inside the small common room and kitchen area. Owners Jynell and Jeff Kristal will provide beach towels and chairs. *12 Crocker Ave., Box 1658, 02568, tel. 508/693–1151 or 800/772–0102. 8. Air-conditioning. AE, MC, V. CP. www. crockerhouseinn.com*

$$$ TISBURY INN. At the center of the shopping district, this three-story hotel—dating to 1794—offers tiled bathrooms with tub showers, firm beds, and amenities that include a well-equipped health club (with the only indoor hotel pool on the island), cable TV, air-conditioning, and ceiling fans. Pastel colors, floral fabrics, and simple decor lend the rooms an islandy feel; on the downside, rooms are small and those facing the main street tend to be noisy. No. 32's windows on two walls let in plenty of sunshine and allow a smidgen of a view of the harbor. Look for special packages in summer. *9 Main St., Box 428, 02568, tel. 508/693–2200 or 800/332–4112, fax 508/693–4095. www.tisburyinn.com 28 rooms, 4 suites. Restaurant, indoor pool, health club. No pets, no smoking. AE, D, DC, MC, V. CP.*

$ ⚠ Martha's Vineyard Family Campground. Wooded sites, a ★ ball field, camp store, bicycle rentals, and electrical and water hookups are among the facilities at this 20-acre campsite located a couple of miles from Vineyard Haven. A step up from tents are 12 rustic one- or two-room cabins, which come with combinations of double and bunk beds (but bring your own bedding) and with electricity, refrigerators, and gas grills. The campground also has hookups for trailers. This is the only campsite on the island, so book early. Discounts are available for extended stays. No dogs or motorcycles are allowed. *569 Edgartown–Vineyard Haven Rd., Box 1557, 02568, tel. 508/693–3772, fax 508/693–5767. 180 sites, 12 cabins. Picnic area, refrigerators (some), bicycles, shop, recreation room, playground, coin laundry. D, MC, V. Closed mid-Oct.–mid-May. www.campmvfc.com*

OAK BLUFFS

$$$ **OAK HOUSE.** The wraparound veranda of this pastel-painted
★ 1872 Victorian looks across a busy street to the beach. Several rooms have private terraces; if you're bothered by noise, ask for a room at the back. Inside, the reason for the inn's name becomes clear: everywhere you look you will see richly patinaed oak in ceilings, wall paneling, wainscoting, and furnishings. All this well-preserved wood creates an appropriate setting for the choice antique furniture and nautical-theme accessories. An elegant afternoon tea with cakes and cookies is served in a glassed-in sunporch. With its white wicker, plants, floral-print pillows, and original stained-glass window accents, it's a lovely place to while away the end of the day. *75 Sea View Ave., Box 299, 02557, tel. 508/ 693–4187 or 800/245–5979, fax 508/696–7385. 8 rooms, 2 suites. No pets, no smoking, no children under 10. AE, D, MC, V. Closed mid-Oct.– mid-May. CP.*

$$–$$$ **ADMIRAL BENBOW INN.** Located on a busy road between Vineyard Haven and Oak Bluffs Harbor, and spruced up with blue-gray paint and a new porch, the Benbow is endearing. The small B&B was built for a minister at the turn of the century, and it is decked out with elaborate woodwork, a comfortable hodgepodge of antique furnishings, and a Victorian parlor with a stunning tile-and-carved-wood fireplace. The rooms are much the same, an eclectic mix of antiques and your grandmother's favorite comfy furniture. Guests have access to an ice machine and refrigerator in the kitchen. Next door to the rather drab yard is a gas station, but the price is right, and the location a few blocks from the harbor is convenient and children are welcome. Manager Joyce Dodge serves a Continental-plus breakfast that includes seasonal fruit, yogurt, and homemade cereal. *81 New York Ave., Box 2488, 02557, tel. 508/693–6825, fax 508/696–6191. 6 rooms. No smoking. AE, D, MC, V. CP.*

$$$ DOCKSIDE INN. Just yards from the Oak Bluffs ferry and in the thick of the town's bustle, the modern Dockside is a good bet for folks who want to be close to the action. The pink lobby and rich florals of the rooms might be a bit vivid for some, but the overall ambience is warm. Kids are welcome, and they'll have plenty to do in town and at nearby beaches. Rooms that open onto building-length balconies have air-conditioning, cable TV, and reproduction antique furniture; some have full kitchens or kitchenettes. A small cottage at the back of the main building, the inn's quiet spot, houses two suites (one with hot tub, both with private decks) and a roof-top widow's walk. There's no restaurant here, but several are within walking distance. *9 Circuit Ave. Ext., Box 1206, 02557, tel. 508/693–2966 or 800/245–5979, fax 508/696–7293. 17 rooms, 5 suites. AE, D, MC, V. Closed late Oct.–Mar. CP.*

$$$ PEQUOT HOTEL. All the bustle of downtown Oak Bluffs is a pleasant five-minute walk past Carpenter Gothic houses from this casual cedar-shingle inn. The furniture won't win any prizes, but the old wing has a bit more atmosphere (if TV is important to you, make sure to request a room in the new wing, as there are none in the older section). In the main section of the building, the first floor has a wide porch with rocking chairs—perfect for getting in some reading and for enjoying coffee or tea with the cookies that are set out in the afternoon—and a small breakfast room where you help yourself to bagels, muffins, and cereal in the morning. The rooms here tend to be more functional, modern, and motel-like. The hotel is one block from the beaches that line the Oak Bluffs–Edgartown Road. Weekend rates are higher than weekday rates. *19 Pequot Ave., 02557, tel. 508/693–5087 or 800/947–*

oak bluffs lodging

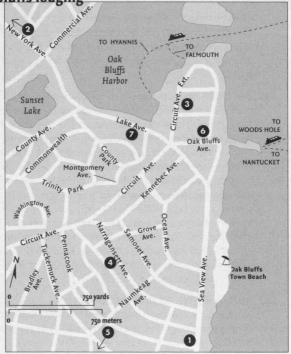

Admiral Benbow Inn, 2

Attleboro House, 7

Dockside Inn, 3

MV Surfside Motel, 6

Oak House, 1

Pequot Hotel, 4

Sea Spray Inn, 5

8704, fax 508/696–9413. 29 rooms, 1 3-bedroom apartment. Breakfast room. AE, MC, V. Closed mid-Oct.–Apr. CP. www.pequothotel.com

$$$ MARTHA'S VINEYARD SURFSIDE MOTEL. These two buildings stand right in the thick of things, so it tends to get noisy in summer. Rooms are spacious and bright (corner rooms more so), and many have been recently upgraded with new carpets, wallpaper, and tile floors; each comes with typical motel furnishings and a table and chairs. Deluxe rooms have water views. Four suites have whirlpool baths, while two are wheelchair-accessible. Midweek rates are reduced by $10–$20. *70 Oak Bluffs Ave., Box 2507, 02557, tel. 508/693–2500 or 800/537–3007, fax 508/693–7343. 34 rooms, 4 suites. AE, D, MC, V. www.mvsurfside.com*

$$–$$$ SEA SPRAY INN. Carol Dennis's porch-wrapped Victorian B&B overlooks expansive Waban Park, with views of the ocean beyond. The rooms are outfitted with new king-size, four-poster feather beds and other personal touches. Room 3's iron-and-brass bed is positioned for viewing the sunrise through windows draped in lacy curtains, and the cedar-lined bath includes an extralarge shower. The garden-side Room 1 has a four-poster bed and a private enclosed porch. Public tennis and the beach are within walking distance. *2 Naumkeag Ave., Box 2355, 02557, tel. 508/693–9388, fax 508/696–7765. 5 rooms, 3 with bath, 2 suites;. No smoking, no children under 12. MC, V. Closed Dec.–Apr. CP.*

$ ATTLEBORO HOUSE. This guest house, part of the Methodist Association Camp Grounds, is across the street from bustling Oak Bluffs Harbor. The big 1874 gingerbread Victorian, an inn since its construction, has wraparound verandas on two floors and small, simple rooms with powder-blue walls, lacy white curtains, and a few antiques. Some rooms have sinks. Singles have three-quarter beds, and every room is provided linen exchange but no chambermaid service during a stay. The five shared baths are rustic and old but clean. *42 Lake Ave., Box 1564, 02557, tel. 508/693–4346. 9 rooms without bath. AE, MC, V. Closed Oct.–mid-May. CP.*

148

EDGARTOWN

$$$$ **CHARLOTTE INN.** From the moment you walk up to the dark-wood
★ Scottish barrister's desk at check-in you'll be surrounded by the
trappings and customs of a bygone era. Guests' names are
handwritten into the register by the dignified and attentive staff.
Beautiful antique furnishings, *objets*, and paintings fill the property—
the book you pick up in your room might be an 18th-century edition
of Voltaire, and your bed could be a hand-carved four-poster. All
rooms have hair dryers, phones, robes, and (except for one room)
TVs. This elegant atmosphere extends to the outstanding restaurant
L'étoile (☞ Chapter 3). *27 S. Summer St., 02539, tel. 508/627–4751,
fax 508/627–4652. 23 rooms and 2 suites in 5 buildings. Restaurant, library.
No children under 14. AE, MC, V. CP. www.charlotteinn.com*

$$$$ **HARBOR VIEW HOTEL.** The centerpiece of this historic hotel is a
★ gray-shingle, 1891 Victorian building with wraparound veranda and
a gazebo. Accommodations are also in a complex of buildings in
the rear that take up a great chunk of a residential neighborhood
a few minutes from downtown. Town houses have cathedral
ceilings, decks, kitchens, and large living areas with sofa beds.
Rooms in other buildings, however, very much resemble upscale
motel rooms, so ask for main-building or town-house rooms for
more colorful lodgings. A beach, good for walking, stretches ¾ mi
from the hotel's dock, and the sheltered bay is a great place for
kids to swim. The hotel's Coach House restaurant, with great
views of Edgartown Light and Chappaquiddick, is one of the finest
in town. Packages and theme weekends, as well as rooms with
kitchenettes, are available. *131 N. Water St., Box 7, 02539, tel. 508/
627–7000 or 800/225–6005, fax 508/627–7845. 102 rooms, 22 suites.
Restaurant, kitchenettes (some), room service, pool, 2 tennis courts, dock,
laundry service, concierge. AE, DC, MC, V. www.harbor-view.com*

$$$$ **KELLEY HOUSE.** At the center of town, this sister property of the
Harbor View (☞ *above*) combines services and amenities with a
country-inn feel. The 1742 white clapboard main house and the
adjacent Garden House are surrounded by pink roses; inside, the

decor is an odd mix of country French and Shaker. Large suites in the Chappaquiddick House and the two spacious town houses with full kitchens in the Wheel House have porches (most with harbor views) and living rooms. All guest rooms have cable TVs, phones, and air-conditioning. The 1742 pub, with original hand-hewn timbers and ballast-brick walls, serves light fare and microbrewed beers on tap. *23 Kelly St., Box 37, 02539, tel. 508/627–7900 or 800/225–6005, fax 508/627–8142. 42 rooms, 9 suites, 2 town-house units. Pub, pool, 2 tennis courts, baby-sitting, laundry service. AE, DC, MC, V. Closed Nov.–Apr. CP. www.kelly-house.com*

$$$$ **MATTAKESETT.** The Mattakesett resort purchased the inn across the road and redubbed it the Winnetu. Now the enormous resort complex, at windswept Katama, consists of Mattakesett's individually owned three- and four-bedroom homes and town houses and Winnetu's studios, condominiums, and suites, all within walking distance of South Beach. Both sets of accommodations share facilities, including the South Beach Cafe. All Mattakesett homes are spacious, sleep eight, and have phones, full kitchens with dishwashers, washer-dryers, fireplaces, and decks (some with bay and ocean views). The children's programs and facilities have been expanded, and the pool and barbecue grills add to the family atmosphere. Bookings at Mattakesett are taken on a per-week basis only and at Winnetu for three, four, or seven nights. For information and bookings, call the off-island reservations number weekdays. *Katama Rd., 02539, tel. 508/627–8920, fax 508/627–7015; reservations c/o Stanmar Corp., 130 Boston Post Rd., Sudbury, MA 01776, tel. 978/443–1733, fax 978/443–0479. 92 units at Mattakesett, 48 units at Winnetu. Restaurant, kitchenettes, 2 pools, 8 tennis courts, aerobics, children's programs (ages 3–13). No credit cards at Mattakesett; MC, V at Winnetu. Mattakesett closed Columbus Day–Memorial Day, Winnetu closed Dec.–March. www.mattakesett.com*

$$$–$$$$ **SHIVERICK INN.** This elegant inn is set in a striking 1840 former doctor's home with mansard roof and cupola. Rooms are airy and bright, with high ceilings; lots of windows, America, English, and

edgartown lodging

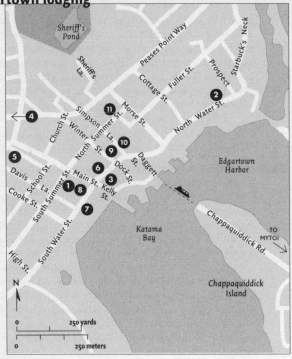

Charlotte Inn, 1

Colonial Inn, 9

Daggett House, 10

Edgartown Commons, 11

Harbor View Hotel, 2

Harborside Inn, 7

Kelly House, 3

Mattakesett, 4

Shiverick Inn, 5

Tuscany Inn, 6

Victorian Inn, 8

eclectic antiques; and rich fabrics and wallpapers. Beds are queen-size with canopies or carved four-posters, and nine rooms have fireplaces or woodstoves. A full breakfast is served in a lovely summerhouse-style room with a wood-burning fireplace. There's a second-floor library with cable TV and a stereo, as well as a terrace and a first-floor flagstone garden patio. The inn's public phone is by the front desk. The heart of downtown is about a five-minute walk. *5 Peases Point Way, at Pent La., Box 640, 02539, tel. 508/627-3797 or 800/723-4292, fax 508/627-8441. 10 rooms. No smoking, no children under 12. AE, D, MC, V. BP.*

$$$$ TUSCANY INN. Inspired by the eponymous region, the inn combines European sophistication and New England style, rather like an Italian villa with Victorian leanings. Rooms are decorated with fine fabrics and treasures that the owners have collected. The inn has king, queen, and twin accommodations; some baths have whirlpool tubs and harbor views. Guests can mingle in front of the fire in the parlor, read on the veranda, or munch on homemade biscotti on the patio in the side yard, surrounded by lovely gardens and twinkling white lights. Breakfast, which may include frittatas, fresh-baked bread, and fresh fruit, is a highlight, and dining in the intimate La Cucina restaurant will make you feel as if you're in Italy. *22 N. Water St., Box 2428, 02539, tel. 508/627-5999, fax 508/627-6605. 8 rooms. AE, DC, MC, V. Closed Jan.–Mar. BP.*

$$$–$$$$ HARBORSIDE INN. Right on the harbor, with boat docks at the end of a landscaped lawn, the large inn offers a central location, harbor-view decks, and plenty of amenities. Seven buildings sprawl around formal rose beds, brick walkways, a patio, and a heated pool. Rooms have Colonial-style furnishings, brass beds and lamps, textured wallpapers, and cable TV. *3 S. Water St., Box 67, 02539, tel. 508/627-4321 or 800/627-4009, fax 508/627-7566. 89 rooms, 3 suites. Air-conditioning, refrigerators, pool, hot tub, sauna. AE, MC, V. Closed mid-Nov.–mid-Apr.*

$$$–$$$$ VICTORIAN INN. White with the classic black shutters of the
★ town's historic homes and fronted by ornate columns, this
appropriately named inn a block from the downtown harbor area
was built as the home of 19th-century whaling captain Lafayette
Rowley. Today the inn's three floors are done in dark woods and
bold floral wallpapers, with rugs over wood floors. Several rooms
hold handmade reproduction four-poster beds, while others have
quiet vestibules and balconies; the French doors of No. 11 open
for wide views of the harbor and Chappaquiddick Island. Breakfast,
served in the garden, includes creative muffins and breads.
Bottled water is in all rooms, and a glass of cream sherry greets
all arrivals. 24 S. Water St., 02539, tel. 508/627–4784. 14 rooms. No
children under 8. MC, V. BP. www.thevic.com

$$$ COLONIAL INN. The inn, part of a complex of shops, is perfect if
★ you like having modern conveniences and being at the center of
the action. Rooms are decorated in soft floral peaches or pastel blues
and yellows, with white pine furniture, wall-to-wall carpeting in most
rooms, and brass beds and lamps, each with a good-size bathroom;
suites have sofa beds. The cable TV system in the inn has been
upgraded, as has the lobby, which is now brightened with light paints
and a large hearth. Several common upper-floor decks are great
for relaxing, and the fourth-floor deck has a superb view of the harbor.
Several newer rooms with private decks also have excellent views.
Holiday theme weekends, celebrating Halloween and Thanksgiving,
are family-friendly, and you'd be hard-pressed to find a more
informative and attentive staff anywhere on the island. 38 N. Water
St., Box 68, 02539, tel. 508/627–4711 or 800/627–4701, fax 508/627–
5904. 39 rooms, 2 suites, 2 efficiencies. Restaurant. AE, MC, V. Closed
Dec.–Apr. CP. www.colonialinnmvy.com

$$$ DAGGETT HOUSE. The flower-bordered lawn that separates the
★ main house from the harbor makes a great retreat after a day of
exploring town, a minute away. All four inn buildings are decorated
with fine wallpapers, antiques, and reproductions (including some
canopy beds). Much of the buildings' historical ambience has been

preserved, including a secret stairway that's now a private entrance to an upstairs guest room. The Widow's Walk Suite has a full kitchen and a private roof walk with a superb water view and a hot tub. Six other rooms have kitchenettes, and another has a hot tub; some have TVs. Breakfast and dinner are served in the 1660 tavern. *59 N. Water St., Box 1333, 02539, tel. 508/627–4600 or 800/946–3400, fax 508/627–4611. 27 rooms, 4 suites. No smoking. AE, D, MC, V.*

\$\$\$ EDGARTOWN COMMONS. This condominium complex of seven buildings, which includes an old house and motel rooms around a busy pool, is just a couple of blocks from town. Studios and one- or two-bedroom condos all have full kitchens, and some are very spacious. Each has been decorated by its individual owner, so the decor varies. None have phones. Family-oriented, the place buzzes with lots of kids; rooms away from the pool are quieter. *20 Peases Point Way, Box 1293, 02539, tel. 508/627–4671 or 800/439–4671 (eastern Mass. only), fax 508/627–4271. 35 units. Picnic area, pool, playground, coin laundry. AE, MC, V. Closed mid-Oct.–Apr.*

UP-ISLAND

WEST TISBURY

\$\$\$–\$\$\$\$ LAMBERT'S COVE COUNTRY INN. A narrow road winds through ★ pine woods to this secluded inn, surrounded by gardens and old stone walls. Rooms in the 1790 farmhouse have floral wallpapers and a country feel. Rooms in outbuildings have porches or decks. Among the common areas is a library with fireplace. At the restaurant, the soft candlelight and excellent Continental cooking make it a destination for a special dinner, whether you stay the night or not. *Off Lambert's Cove Rd., W. Tisbury; mailing address: R.R. 1, Box 422, Vineyard Haven 02568, tel. 508/693–2298, fax 508/693–7890. 15 rooms. Restaurant, tennis court, library. AE, MC, V. BP.*

\$\$–\$\$\$ BAYBERRY BED AND BREAKFAST. If you have an urge to spend time in the bucolic Up-Island countryside, Rosalie Powell's B&B is the place for you. The farmhouse-style home sits on land owned by Rosalie's family, descended from Thomas Mayhew, the founder of the island. The rooms are decorated in a country Victorian style, with lots of blue highlights in the rugs, trim, and wallpapers. Two rooms on the first floor share a bath, while the three upstairs rooms have private or semi-private (designated for the room, but in the hall) baths. The sitting room has comfy chairs, a fireplace, and a piano decorated with photos of Rosalie's family, but the heart of the inn is the big kitchen, which has a hearth and glass doors opening to a cherry tree–shaded brick patio and, beyond, an apple orchard and herb garden. Don't miss Rosalie's famous breakfast Dreamboat, a boat-shaped pastry filled with fresh fruit, yogurt, honey, and granola. *49 Old Courthouse Rd., Box 654, 02575, tel. 508/693–1984 or 800/693–9960, fax 508/693–4505. 5 rooms, 3 with bath. No children under 12. AE, MC, V. Closed Jan.–Feb. BP.*

$ HOSTELLING INTERNATIONAL–MARTHA'S VINEYARD. The only budget alternative in season, this hostel is one of the country's best. The large kitchen is outfitted with multiple refrigerators and stoves (barbecue grills are available, too), the common room has a fireplace and plenty of books, and local events on the bulletin board. Morning chores are required in summer. The hostel offers summer programs on island history, as well as nature tours. It is near a bike path and is 2 mi from the airport and about 3 mi from the nearest beach. The Island Shuttle makes a stop out front. *Edgartown–West Tisbury Rd., Box 158, 02575, tel. 508/693–2665 or 617/779–0900. 78 dorm-style beds. Volleyball, coin laundry. MC, V. 11 PM curfew June–Aug. Closed daytime 10–5 and completely Nov.–Apr. www.hi-travel.org*

CHILMARK

$$$$ INN AT BLUEBERRY HILL. Exclusive and secluded, this cedar-shingle retreat and its 56 acres of former farmland put you in the heart of the rural Vineyard. The restaurant is relaxed and elegant, and the fresh, health-conscious food is thoughtfully prepared. A cold breakfast is included in the room rate, and a box lunch is available for a picnic on the beach (a guest shuttle runs to Lucy

ONE LAST TRAVEL TIP:

Pack an easy way to reach the world.

123 456 7891 2345
J.D. SMITH

Wherever you travel, the MCI WorldCom Card℠ is the easiest way to stay in touch. You can use it to call to and from more than 125 countries worldwide. And you can earn bonus miles every time you use your card. So go ahead, travel the world. MCI WorldCom℠ makes it even more rewarding. For additional access codes, visit **www.wcom.com/worldphone**.

MCI WORLDCOM.

EASY TO CALL WORLDWIDE

1. Just dial the WorldPhone® access number of the country you're calling from.

2. Dial or give the operator your MCI WorldCom Card number.

3. Dial or give the number you're calling.

Belgium ◆	0800-10012
Czech Republic ◆	00-42-000112
Denmark ◆	8001-0022

France ◆	0-800-99-0019
Germany	0800-888-8000
Hungary ◆	06▼-800-01411
Ireland	1-800-55-1001
Italy ◆	172-1022
Mexico	01-800-021-8000
Netherlands ◆	0800-022-91-22
Spain	900-99-0014
Switzerland ◆	0800-89-0222
United Kingdom	0800-89-0222
United States	1-800-888-8000

◆ Public phones may require deposit of coin or phone card for dial tone.   ▼ Wait for second dial tone.

EARN FREQUENT FLIER MILES

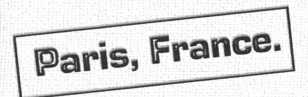

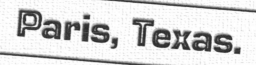

When it Comes to Getting Cash at an ATM, Same Thing.

Whether you're in Yosemite or Yemen, using your Visa® card or ATM card with the PLUS symbol is the easiest and most convenient way to get cash. Even if your bank is in Minneapolis and you're in Miami, Visa/PLUS ATMs make getting cash so easy, you'll feel right at home. After all, Visa/PLUS ATMs are open 24 hours a day, 7 days a week, rain or shine. And if you need help finding one of Visa's 627,000 ATMs in 127 countries worldwide, visit **visa.com/pd/atm**. We'll make finding an ATM as easy as finding the Eiffel Tower, the Pyramids or even the Grand Canyon.

It's Everywhere You Want To Be.®

Vincent and Squibnocket beaches). Guest rooms are tastefully decorated with Shaker-inspired, island-made furniture, and beds are fitted with handmade mattresses with all-cotton sheets and duvets. Most rooms have glass doors that open onto terraces or private decks set with Adirondack chairs. There is a large parlor-library with a fireplace and a casual den and fitness center. Less expensive rooms may be small, and consider whether you'd prefer staying upstairs in the main building or in one of the three detached cottages. Also note that rooms can be combined to create two- or three-bedroom suites. *74 North Rd., R.R. 1, Box 309, Chilmark 02535, tel. 508/645–3322 or 800/356–3322, fax 508/645–3799. 25 rooms. Dining room, air-conditioning, lap pool, massage, tennis court, exercise room, meeting room, airport shuttle. AE, MC, V. Closed Nov.–Apr. CP. www.blueberryinn.com*

MENEMSHA

$$$–$$$$ ★ **MENEMSHA INN AND COTTAGES.** For 40 years the *Life* photographer Alfred Eisenstaedt returned to his cottage on the hill here for the panoramic view of Vineyard Sound and Cuttyhunk beyond the trees below. All with screened porches, fireplaces, and full kitchens, the cottages are nicely spaced on 10 acres and vary in privacy and view. You can also stay in the 1989 inn building or in the pleasant Carriage House, both of which have Appalachian reproduction furniture. All rooms and suites have private decks, with sunset views, as well as phones and cable TV. Suites include sitting areas, desks, mini-refrigerators, and big tiled baths. The Continental breakfast is available at the inn and Carriage House only. *North Rd., Box 38, 02552, tel. 508/645–2521. 9 rooms, 6 suites, 12 cottages, 1 3-bedroom house. Tennis court, exercise room. No pets. No credit cards. Closed Dec.–mid-Apr. CP. www.menemshainn.com*

AQUINNAH

$$$$ ★ **OUTERMOST INN.** Hugh and Jeanne Taylor's B&B by the Aquinnah Cliffs takes full advantage of the location: standing alone on acres of moorland, the house is wrapped in windows revealing

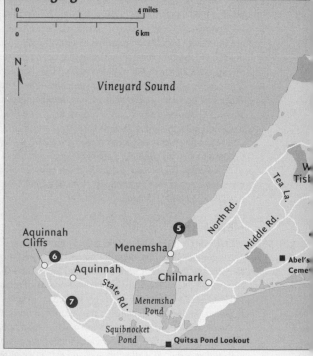

Bayberry
B&B, 2

Duck Inn, 7

Hostelling
International, 3

Inn at Blueberry
Hill, 4

Lambert's Cove
Country Inn, 1

Menemsha
Inn, 5

Outermost
Inn, 6

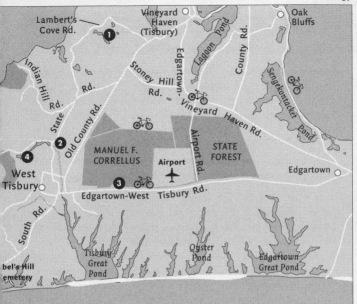

Lambert's
Cove Rd.

Vineyard
Haven
(Tisbury)

Oak
Bluffs

Indian Hill
Rd.

State

Rd.

Stoney Hill
Rd.

Edgartown-

Lagoon Pond

County Rd.

Sengekontacket Pond

Vineyard

Haven Rd.

Old County Rd.

MANUEL F.
CORRELLUS

Airport

Airport Rd.

STATE
FOREST

Edgartown

West
Tisbury

West Tisbury

Edgartown-West

Tisbury Rd.

South Rd.

bel's Hill
emetery

Tisbury
Great
Pond

Oyster
Pond

Edgartown
Great
Pond

ATLANTIC OCEAN

Renting a House or Condo

Apartment, condo, or house rentals are a good bet for families or groups who plan to stay for at least a week and have a hankering to retain a greater degree of autonomy than is afforded by resorts and B&Bs. You can cook, eat, see the sights, and sleep at your leisure. The accommodations vary wildly, from town efficiency apartments to large, seaside two- or three-bedroom condo complexes and multibedroom mansions. The rates vary according to size, amenities offered, and location—in general, the closer to the ocean, the more expensive the accommodation.

Most often, renters will find condos and homes well outfitted, with full kitchens, including a refrigerator and microwave, TV with VCR, air-conditioning and fans, barbecue equipment, and bedding. Beach towels, chairs, umbrellas, and parking stickers for local beaches might also be available, but don't expect daily or even weekly maid service. You can often request it, at extra charge. Some renters will stock the refrigerator for you (at your cost), as long as you provide a list.

Weekly rentals usually work on a Saturday-to-Saturday or, in some cases, Monday-to-Monday basis. Most accept credit cards. The key to getting what you want in a rental is to book early; also ask direct questions about what amenities and services are offered and what you might need to bring to make your stay comfortable. Also ask, if applicable, about children and pets.

There are hundreds of rental properties on Martha's Vineyard, and most can be found in local newspapers or through a number of local rental agencies. A recent sampling of summer-season rental rates found these properties: a four-bedroom, three-bath contemporary in Katama for $2,750 per week; a studio apartment in West Tisbury for $800 per week; a four-bedroom, four-bath house on the beach in Oak Bluffs for $6,600 per week; a three-bedroom contemporary near the beach in Aquinnah for $2,000 per week.

views of sea and sky in three directions. A wide porch and new patio extends along the back side of the house, providing great views of the Aquinnah Lighthouse. The expanded restaurant, open to the public, serves dinner four to six nights a week from spring through fall. Dinners are all prix-fixe at $60 (reservations are essential, and it's BYOB). The decor of the inn is clean and contemporary, with white walls and polished light-wood floors. Each room has a phone, and one has a whirlpool tub. The beach is a 10-minute walk away. Hugh has sailed area waters since childhood and captains his 50-ft catamaran on excursions to Cuttyhunk Island. *Lighthouse Rd., R.R. 1, Box 171, 02535, tel. 508/645–3511, fax 508/645–3514. 7 rooms. Restaurant. No pets, no children under 12. AE, D, MC, V. Closed mid-Oct.–May. BP. www.outermostinn.com*

$$–$$$ **DUCK INN.** Elise LeBovit's Duck Inn, originally an 18th-century
★ home built by Native American seafarer George Belain, sits on a bucolic 5-acre bluff overlooking the ocean, with the Aquinnah Lighthouse standing sentinel to the north. The only sounds at night are crickets and the ocean surf. The eclectic, fun decor blends peach stucco walls, Native American rugs and wall hangings, and ducks. The duck sign on State Road that directs you to the inn's winding dirt track is just one clue that Elise is big on waterfowl. Three upstairs rooms come with balconies, a suite in the stone-wall lower level (cool in summer, warm in winter) offers views of the rolling fields, and a small attached cabin with separate bath is the least expensive room. The first floor's common room, with a working 1928 Glenwood stove, piano, and fireplace, is the heart of the inn. Massage and facial therapies are available, and the healthy breakfast fare includes waffles with strawberries and omelets, or the more decadent chocolate crepes. This inn is very informal, kids and pets are welcome, and one night is free with a week's stay. *State Rd., Box 160, 02535, tel. 508/645–9018, fax 508/645–2790. 4 rooms, 1 suite. Outdoor hot tub. MC, V. BP.*

PRACTICAL INFORMATION

Air Travel

BOOKING YOUR FLIGHT

When you book, **look for nonstop flights** and **remember that "direct" flights stop at least once.** Try to **avoid connecting flights,** which require a change of plane. Two airlines may operate a connecting flight, so ask if your airline operates every segment. Your preferred carrier may fly you only part of the way.

Ask your airline if it offers electronic ticketing, which eliminates all or most paperwork. There's no ticket to pick up or misplace. You go directly to the gate and give the agent your confirmation number.

➤ AIRLINES AND CONTACTS: **Air New England** (tel. 508/693–8899) offers an island-based charter service year-round. **Cape Air/Nantucket Airlines** (tel. 508/771–6944 or 800/352–0714, www.flycapeair.com) connects the Vineyard year-round with Boston (including an hourly summer shuttle), Hyannis, Nantucket, and New Bedford. It offers joint fares and ticketing and baggage agreements with several major carriers. **Continental Express** (tel. 800/525–0280) has seasonal nonstop flights to the Vineyard from Newark, New Jersey. **Direct Flight** (tel. 508/693–6688) is a year-round charter service based on the Vineyard. **Ocean Wings** (tel. 508/693–4646 or 800/253–5039) flies to and from New England cities and New York. **US Airways Express** (tel. 800/428–4322) has year-round service to the Vineyard, as well as Hyannis and Nantucket, out of Boston and New York City's LaGuardia Airport, and seasonal service from Washington, D.C. **Westchester Air** (tel. 800/759–2929) flies charters out of White Plains, New York.

FLYING TIMES

Flying time is one hour from New York, 30 minutes from Boston, 25 minutes from Providence, 15 minutes from Hyannis.

AIRPORT INFORMATION

The renovated **Martha's Vineyard Airport** (Edgartown–West Tisbury Rd., tel. 508/693–7022) is in West Tisbury, about 5 mi west of Edgartown.

Boat and Ferry Travel

BY PRIVATE BOAT

Town harbor facilities are available at **Vineyard Haven** (tel. 508/696–4249), **Oak Bluffs** (tel. 508/693–4355), **Edgartown** (tel. 508/627–4746), and **Menemsha** (tel. 508/645–2846). Private marine companies include **Vineyard Haven Marina** (tel. 508/693–0720), **Dockside Marina** (tel. 508/693–3392) in Oak Bluffs, and **Edgartown Marine** (tel. 508/627–4388).

BY FERRY

The three-car **On Time** (Dock St., Edgartown, tel. 508/627–9427) ferry—so named because it has no printed schedules and therefore can never be late—makes the five-minute run to Chappaquiddick Island year-round; Memorial Day to mid-October it runs about every five minutes daily 7 AM to midnight, less frequently off-season. Round-trip fares are as follows: individual $1.50, car and driver $6, bicycle and rider $4, moped and rider $5.50, motorcycle and rider $5.

Car-and-passenger ferries travel to Vineyard Haven from Woods Hole on Cape Cod year-round. In season, passenger ferries from Falmouth and Hyannis on Cape Cod, and from New Bedford, serve Vineyard Haven and Oak Bluffs. All provide parking lots where you can leave your car overnight ($7–$12 per night).

➤ **FROM WOODS HOLE:** The **Steamship Authority** (tel. 508/477–8600 for information and car reservations; 508/693–9130 on the Vineyard; 508/540–1394 TTY for information and car reservations; 508/548–3788 for day-of-sailing information, www.islandferry.com) runs the only car ferries, which make the 45-minute trip to Vineyard Haven daily year-round and to Oak Bluffs from late May through September.

If you plan to take a car to the island in summer, you must have a reservation (specifically Memorial Day Weekend, Friday through Monday from the end of June to mid-September, and every day for the first two weeks of July). Standby reservations are otherwise available, but make it easy on yourself and get an advance reservation, whenever you travel during the summer. Passenger reservations are never necessary. You should book your car reservation as far ahead as possible; in season, call weekdays from 5 AM to 9:55 PM for faster service. Those with confirmed car reservations must be at the terminal 30 minutes (45 minutes in season) before sailing time.

The one-way year-round fee for passengers is $5; bicycles are $3. For cars, the one-way in-season (mid-May–mid-October) fee is $49 per car (not including passengers). Call for off-season rates.

A number of **parking lots** in Falmouth hold the overflow of cars when the Woods Hole lot is filled, and free shuttle buses take passengers to the ferry, about 15 minutes away. Signs along Route 28 heading south from the Bourne Bridge direct you to open parking lots, as does AM radio station 1610, which can be picked up within 5 mi of Falmouth.

A free **Martha's Vineyard Chamber of Commerce reservations phone** at the ticket office in Woods Hole connects you with many lodgings and car- and moped-rental firms on the island.

Tickets may be purchased through the contacts numbers above or through Plymouth and Brockton as well as Bonanza bus terminals (☞ *below*).

➤ FROM HYANNIS: Hy-Line (Ocean St. dock, tel. 508/778–2600 or 888/778–1132; 508/778–2602 for reservations; 508/693–0112 in Oak Bluffs; www.hy-linecruises.com) makes the 1¾-hour run to Oak Bluffs May to October. The one-way per-person fee is $12.50; bicycles are $5. From June to mid-September, Hy-Line also carries passengers between Oak Bluffs and Nantucket (one-way $12.50, bikes $5, 2¼ hours). The parking lot fills up in summer, so call to reserve a space in high season. Note: this is not a car ferry.

➤ **FROM FALMOUTH: Falmouth Ferry Service** (Falmouth Harbor, tel. 508/548–9400) makes the one-hour trip to Edgartown late May through Columbus Day weekend. During the height of summer, the passenger ferry runs daily, weekends in the slower months. Reservations are recommended. The round-trip fee is $22, bicycles $6; one-way passengers pay $12.50.

The **Island Queen** (Falmouth Harbor, tel. 508/548–4800, www.islandqueen.com) makes the 35-minute trip to Oak Bluffs from late May through Columbus Day. The round-trip fee is $10, $6 for bicycles; the one-way fee is $6, $3 for bicycles. No passenger reservations are necessary.

Patriot Boats (Scranton Ave., Falmouth Harbor, tel. 508/548–2626) allows passengers on its Oak Bluffs mail runs starting with 3:15 AM departures from Falmouth Harbor. Last run is about 4 PM. The boat runs daily in-season, more frequently during off-season, and operates a year-round 24-hour water taxi. Times of the earliest departures of the day aren't guaranteed—these are the newspaper runs, and departure depends on when the papers arrive from Boston. The one-way fee is $6.

➤ **FROM NEW BEDFORD:** The **Schamonchi** (Martha's Vineyard ticket office: Beach Rd., Vineyard Haven, tel. 508/693–2088, tel. 508/997–1688 in New Bedford, www.mvferry.com) travels between Billy Woods Wharf and Vineyard Haven from mid-May to mid-October. The 600-passenger ferry makes the 1½-hour trip at least once a day, several times in high season, allowing you to avoid Cape traffic. Note that round-trip $17 passenger and $5 bicycle fares apply only for same-day travel; overnight stays require the purchase of two one-way tickets (passenger $9.50, bicycle $2.50).

➤ **FROM NEW LONDON: Fox Navigation** (Pier 44, Beach Rd., Vineyard Haven, tel. 888/724–5369) carries passengers between State Pier in New London, Connecticut, and Vineyard Haven from June to early September. The 257-passenger high-speed ferry makes the two-hour trip Friday through Monday only, once per day. There is no deck on the enclosed ferry; passengers sit in either Clipper Class, round-trip $59, or the more expensive Admiral Class, round-trip $89, which has wider seats, water views, and expanded food service.

➤ FROM NANTUCKET: **Hy-Line** (tel. 508/778–2600 in Hyannis; 508/693–0112 in Oak Bluffs; 508/228–3949 on Nantucket; www.hy-linecruises.com) makes 2¼-hour runs to and from Oak Bluffs from early June to mid-September—the only interisland passenger service. (To get a car from Nantucket to the Vineyard, you must return to the mainland and drive from Hyannis to Woods Hole.) The one-way fee is 12.50; bicycles are $5.

Bus Travel to Martha's Vineyard

Bonanza Bus Lines (tel. 508/548–7588 or 800/556–3815 or 888/751–8800, www.bonanzabus.com) travels to the Woods Hole ferry port on Cape Cod from Boston's Logan Airport, Rhode Island, Connecticut, and New York year-round.

Bus Travel Within Martha's Vineyard

BY SHUTTLE BUS

Throughout the year, buses of the **Island Transport Inc.–Yellow Line** company run schedules among Vineyard towns. They pick up the pace from late June to early September, operating about every 15 minutes daily from 6 AM to 12:45 AM between Vineyard Haven (pickup on Union Street in front of the steamship wharf or Pier 44 on Beach Road), Oak Bluffs (by the Civil War statue in Ocean Park), and Edgartown (on Church Street opposite the Old Whaling Church). Shuttle tickets cost $1.75–$2.25 one-way and as much as $3.25 for round-trip excursions among the three towns. An all-day, unlimited pass is $5, and weekly ($15) and monthly ($50) passes are also available. Buses from the Down-Island towns to Aquinnah—stopping at the airport, West Tisbury, Chilmark, and on demand wherever it's safe to do so—run every couple of hours between 9 AM and 5 PM in July and August. At other times, call to confirm. Cost is $1–$5 one-way.

For the current **bus schedule,** call the shuttle hot line (tel. 508/693–1589 or 508/693–0058, www.mvtour.com) or flip through a Steamship Authority schedule.

The big buses of the **Martha's Vineyard Transit Authority (VTA)** run on a summer schedule (mid-May through September), with in-town services and selected routes such as Edgartown to Vineyard Haven, West Tisbury to Chilmark and Aquinnah, and Edgartown to South Beach. The fare is 50¢ per town, with the exception of trips to South Beach, which are $1.50. Three-day passes ($10) and books of $6 worth of passes for $5 are available at the Edgartown Visitors Center and Alley's General Store. You buy books of 50¢ tickets and drop in the appropriate number for your fare—it will never be more than $1.50. Senior citizens and children 12 and under are free. For the latest schedules and fare informations, call the VTA (tel. 508/627–9663 or 508/627–7448, www.vineyardtransit.com).

BY MINIBUS

The **Martha's Vineyard Transit Authority** has three in-town shuttle-bus routes, two in Edgartown and one in Vineyard Haven. One-way fares are $1.50 or less; senior citizens and children 12 and under are free. For information on weekly, monthly, or seasonal passes, call tel. 508/627–9663 or 508/627–7448.

➤ IN EDGARTOWN: From mid-May to mid-September, white-and-purple shuttle buses make a continuous circuit downtown, beginning at free parking lots on the outskirts—at the Triangle off Upper Main Street, at the Edgartown School on Robinson Road (take a right off West Tisbury Road before Upper Main), and on Mayhew Lane. It's well worth taking it to avoid parking headaches in town, and it's cheap (50¢ each way) and convenient. The shuttle buses run every 15 minutes from 7:30 AM to 11:30 PM daily (mid-May–June, 7:30–7) and can be flagged along the route. Service is also available between Vineyard Haven (free parking lot near Cronig's Market) and the steamship terminal. Minibuses run every 15 minutes from the first ferry in the morning to the last ferry at night. Cost is 50¢ each way and seasonal passes are available; senior citizens and kids under 12 ride free.

Shuttle-bus service to South Beach via Herring Creek and Katama roads is available mid-June–mid-September for $1.50 one-way (10-trip pass, $10). Pickup is at the corner of Main and Church streets. In good weather there are frequent pickups daily between 10 and 6:30, every half hour in inclement weather, or you can flag a shuttle bus whenever you see one. In July and August, evening service to and from South Beach runs to 9:45 PM.

Business Hours

MUSEUMS & SIGHTS
Hours for sights vary widely from place to place and from season to season. Some places are staffed by volunteers and have limited hours (a few hours several days a week) even in summer, although major museums and attractions will be open daily in summer. Always check the hours of a place you plan to visit, and call ahead to confirm if you'll be traveling some distance.

SHOPS
Shop hours are generally 9 or 10 to 5, though in high season many tourist-oriented stores stay open until 10 PM or later. Except in the main tourist areas, shops are often closed on Sunday.

Car Rental

You can book rentals through the Woods Hole ferry terminal free phone. The agencies listed below have rental desks at the airport. Cars rented from the airport incur a surcharge.

GASOLINE
Gasoline stations dot the island roads, but gas prices, due to importing costs, are higher than on the mainland, by as much as 10¢–15¢ per gallon. Stations operate in the same ways they do on the mainland; some are full service, while others are pump-your-own. Hours vary, with most staying open until 10 PM or later.

PARKING

Parking is tight in the main Vineyard towns of Edgartown, Oak Bluffs, and Vineyard Haven. Public parking is found on streets and in some public lots (off Cromwell Street in Vineyard Haven, across from Kelly Street and Dock Street in Edgartown). Cars illegally parked will be ticketed and, in cases, towed, and laws are strictly enforced during the busy summer months.

➤ **RENTAL AGENCIES: All Island** (tel. 508/693–6868), **Budget** (tel. 508/693–1911), **Consumer Car and Truck Rental** (tel. 508/696–6636 or 888/902–7433), and **Hertz** (tel. 508/693–2402 or 800/654–3131).

Adventure Rentals (Beach Rd., Vineyard Haven, tel. 508/693–1959) rents cars (through Thrifty), as well as mopeds, Jeeps, and buggies, and offers half-day rates. Cost is $40–$65 per day for a basic car. **Atlantic Rent-A-Car** (15 Beach Rd., Vineyard Haven, tel. 508/693–0480) rents cars, Jeeps, vans, and convertibles. **Classic Car Rentals** (tel. 508/693–5551) rents classic Corvettes, a '57 Chevy, luxury Jaguars and Porsches and other cars, as well as Harley-Davidson motorcycles, mopeds, and mountain bikes.

INSURANCE

When driving a rented car, you are generally responsible for any damage to or loss of the vehicle as well as for any property damage or personal injury that you may cause. Before you rent see what coverage your personal auto-insurance policy and credit cards already provide.

For about $15–$20 per day, rental companies sell protection, known as a collision- or loss-damage waiver (CDW or LDW), that eliminates your liability for damage to the car.

In Massachusetts the car-rental company must pay for damage to third parties up to a preset legal limit, beyond which your own liability insurance kicks in. However, **make sure you have enough coverage to pay for the car.** If you do not have auto insurance or an umbrella policy that covers damage to third parties, purchasing liability insurance and a CDW or LDW is highly recommended.

REQUIREMENTS & RESTRICTIONS

In Massachusetts you must be 21 to rent a car, and rates may be higher if you're under 25. You might pay extra for child seats, which are compulsory for children under five, and for additional drivers. Non-U.S. residents will need a reservation voucher, a passport, a driver's license, and a travel policy that covers each driver, in order to pick up a car.

SURCHARGES

Before you pick up a car in one town and leave it in another **ask about drop-off charges or one-way service fees,** which can be substantial. Note, too, that some rental agencies charge extra if you return the car before the time specified in your contract. To avoid a hefty refueling fee **fill the tank just before you turn in the car,** but be aware that gas stations near the rental outlet may overcharge. Cars rented at the airport incur a small surcharge imposed by the airport authorities.

Car Travel

In season, the Vineyard is overrun with cars, and many innkeepers will advise you to leave your car at home, saying you won't need it. This is true if you are coming over for just a few days and plan to spend most of your time in the three main towns—Oak Bluffs, Vineyard Haven, and Edgartown—which are connected in summer by a shuttle bus. Otherwise, you'll probably want a car. Driving on the island is fairly simple. There are few main roads, and they are all well marked. Local bookstores sell a number of excellent maps of the island.

BY FOUR-WHEEL-DRIVE

Four-wheel-drive vehicles are allowed from Katama Beach to Wasque Reservation with $50 annual permits ($75 for vehicles not registered on the island) sold on the beach in summer or anytime at the **Dukes County Courthouse** (Treasurer's Office,

Main St., Edgartown 02539, tel. 508/627–4250). Wasque Reservation has a separate mandatory permit (also available at the courthouse) and requires that vehicles carry certain equipment, such as a shovel, tow chains, and rope; call the rangers before setting out for the dunes. Due to the protected status of the piping plover, which uses the shore for nesting, some sections are occasionally closed off to traffic.

Jeeps are a good idea for exploring areas approachable only by dirt roads, but the going can be difficult in over-sand travel, and even Jeeps can get stuck. Stay on existing tracks whenever possible, since wet sand by the water line can suck you in. Most rental companies don't allow their Jeeps to be driven over sand for insurance reasons. Renting a four-wheel-drive vehicle costs $45–$140 per day (seasonal prices fluctuate widely).

Children on Martha's Vineyard

Martha's Vineyard is very family-oriented and provides every imaginable diversion for kids, including lodgings and restaurants that cater to them and that are affordable for families on a budget. Cottages and condominiums are popular with families, offering privacy, room, kitchens, and sometimes laundry facilities. Often cottage or condo communities have play yards and pools, sometimes even full children's programs.

If you rent a car, don't forget to **arrange for a car seat.**

CHILDREN'S ACTIVITIES

The following towns offer recreational programs for children: **Edgartown** (tel. 508/627–6145), **Oak Bluffs** (tel. 508/693–2303), **Vineyard Haven** (tel. 508/696–4200), and **West Tisbury** (tel. 508/696–0147).

Storytelling hours for children are offered by all the island's libraries. Call towns about days and times: **Chilmark** (State Rd., tel. 508/645–3360), **Edgartown** (N. Water St., tel. 508/627–4221), **Oak Bluffs** (Circuit Ave., tel. 508/693–9433), **Vineyard**

Haven (Upper Main St., tel. 508/696–4212), and **West Tisbury** (State Rd., tel. 508/693–3366).

LODGING

Most hotels on Martha's Vineyard allow children under a certain age to stay in their parents' room at no extra charge, but others charge for them as extra adults; be sure to **find out the cutoff age for children's discounts.**

If you're planning to stay at a bed-and-breakfast, be sure to **ask the owners in advance** whether the B&B welcomes children. Some establishments are filled with fragile antiques, and owners may not accept families with children of a certain age.

SIGHTS & ATTRACTIONS

Child-friendly historical, cultural, and natural sights are indicated by a rubber duckie icon (🦆) in the margin.

Dining

The restaurants we list are the cream of the crop in each price category.

RESERVATIONS & DRESS

Reservations are always a good idea: we mention them only when they're essential or are not accepted. Book as far ahead as you can, and reconfirm as soon as you arrive. We mention dress only when men are required to wear a jacket or a jacket and tie.

Disabilities & Accessibility

➤ LOCAL RESOURCES: **Cape Organization for Rights of the Disabled** (CORD; tel. 508/693–4393 in Martha's Vineyard; 508/775–8300 in Hyannis; 800/541–0282 in MA) will supply information on accessibility of restaurants, hotels, beaches, and other tourist facilities on Martha's Vineyard. **Directory of Accessible Facilities** in Massachusetts (www.state.ma.us/dem/access.htm). **Sight Loss Services** (tel. 508/394–3904; 800/334–6842 in MA) provides accessibility and other information and referrals for people with vision impairments. For accessibility information in state parks and beaches, contact the **Massachusetts Department of Environmental Management** (Division of Forests and Parks, 100 Cambridge St., Room 1905, Boston 02202, tel. 617/727–3180, fax 617/727–9402). **Directory of Accessible Facilities** in Massachusetts (www.state.ma.us/dem/access.htm).

LODGING
When discussing accessibility with an operator or reservations agent **ask hard questions.** Are there any stairs, inside or out? Are there grab bars next to the toilet and in the shower/tub? How wide is the doorway to the room? To the bathroom? For the most extensive facilities meeting the latest legal specifications **opt for newer accommodations.**

➤ COMPLAINTS: **Disability Rights Section** (U.S. Department of Justice, Civil Rights Division, Box 66738, Washington, DC 20035-6738, tel. 202/514–0301; 800/514–0301; 202/514–0301 TTY; 800/514–0301 TTY, fax 202/307–1198) for general complaints. **Civil Rights Office** (U.S. Department of Transportation, Departmental Office of Civil Rights, S-30, 400 7th St. SW, Room 10215, Washington, DC 20590, tel. 202/366–4648, fax 202/366–9371) for problems with surface transportation.

Emergencies

Dial **911** for the hospital, physicians, ambulance services, police, fire departments, or Coast Guard.

Martha's Vineyard Hospital (Linton La., Oak Bluffs, tel. 508/693–0410).

Vineyard Medical Services (State Rd., Vineyard Haven, tel. 508/693–6399) provides walk-in care; call for days and hours.

LATE-NIGHT PHARMACY
Leslie's Drug Store (65 Main St., Vineyard Haven, tel. 508/693–1010) is open daily year-round and has a pharmacist on 24-hour call for emergencies.

Gay & Lesbian Travel

Gay and lesbian visitors to Martha's Vineyard will find a generally liberal and sophisticated scene regarding acceptance.

➤ **GAY- AND LESBIAN-FRIENDLY TOUR OPERATORS: New England Vacation Tours** (Box 560, West Dover, VT 05356, tel. 802/464–2076 or 800/742–7669, fax 802/464–2629) offers vacation packages to Martha's Vineyard.

➤ **GAY- AND LESBIAN-FRIENDLY TRAVEL AGENCIES: Corniche Travel** (8721 Sunset Blvd., Suite 200, West Hollywood, CA 90069, tel. 310/854–6000 or 800/429–8747, fax 310/659–7441). **Islanders Kennedy Travel** (183 W. 10th St., New York, NY 10014, tel. 212/242–3222 or 800/988–1181, fax 212/929–8530). **Now Voyager** (4406 18th St., San Francisco, CA 94114, tel. 415/626–1169 or 800/255–6951, fax 415/626–8626). **Yellowbrick Road** (1500 W. Balmoral Ave., Chicago, IL 60640, tel. 773/561–1800 or 800/642–2488, fax 773/561–4497). **Skylink Travel and Tour** (3577 Moorland Ave., Santa Rosa, CA 95407, tel. 707/585–8355 or 800/225–5759, fax 707/584–5637), serving lesbian travelers.

Health

A common problem on the East Coast is Lyme disease. This bacterial infection is transmitted by deer ticks and can be very serious, leading to chronic arthritis and worse if left untreated.

Deer ticks can be found year-round. They are about the size of a pinhead. Anyone planning to explore wooded areas or places with tall grasses (including dunes) should **wear long pants, socks drawn up over pant cuffs, a long-sleeve shirt with a close-fitting collar, and boots.** DEET repellent should be applied to skin (not face!) and permethrin should be applied to clothing directly before entering infested areas.

➤ **LYME DISEASE INFO: Centers for Disease Control** (tel. 404/332–4555) or the **Massachusetts Department of Public Health**

(Southeast Office, 109 Rhode Island Rd., Lakeville, MA 02347, tel. 508/947–1231).

Holidays

Major national holidays include New Year's Day (Jan. 1); Martin Luther King, Jr., Day (3rd Mon. in Jan.); Presidents' Day (3rd Mon. in Feb.); Memorial Day (last Mon. in May); Independence Day (July 4); Labor Day (1st Mon. in Sept.); Thanksgiving Day (4th Thurs. in Nov.); Christmas Eve and Christmas Day (Dec. 24 and 25); and New Year's Eve (Dec. 31). Patriot's Day (3rd Mon. in Apr.) is a Massachusetts state holiday.

Lodging

You can reserve a room at many island establishments via the toll-free phone inside the waiting room at the Woods Hole ferry terminal. The Chamber of Commerce maintains a listing of availability in the peak tourist season, from mid-June to mid-September. During these months, rates are, alas, astronomical, and reservations are essential.

B&BS

Martha's Vineyard and Nantucket Reservations (Box 1322, Lagoon Pond Rd., Vineyard Haven 02568, tel. 508/693–7200; 800/649–5671 in MA) books cottages, apartments, inns, hotels, and B&Bs. **DestINNations** (tel. 508/428–5600 or 800/333–4667) handles a limited number of Vineyard hotels and B&Bs, but the staff will arrange any and all details of a visit.

HOUSE RENTALS

Martha's Vineyard Vacation Rentals (107 Beach Rd., Box 1207, Vineyard Haven 02568, tel. 508/693–7711 or 800/556–4225) and **Sandcastle Vacation Home Rentals** (256 Vineyard Haven Rd., Box 2488, Edgartown 02539, tel. 508/627–5665) can help you find rentals for long-term visits.

Media

The *Martha's Vineyard Times* and *Vineyard Gazette* (publishing since 1846) are the island's two main news organs, and between them you'll have a good idea of island events and happenings. You can find the papers at any bookstore, convenience store, supermarket, or pharmacy on the island. The *Cape Cod Times*, printed in Hyannis, is also available on the island and often carries news of local interest. Local magazines include *Vineyard Home & Garden* and *Times of the Islands*, covering Nantucket as well as the Vineyard. The local radio station is WMVY (92.7 on the dial), an FM album music station, also a good source for concert and nightlife news.

Money Matters

Prices throughout this guide are given for adults. Substantially reduced fees are almost always available for children, students, and senior citizens. For information on taxes, *see* Taxes, *below*.

ATMS

ATM machines are found on the main streets of Edgartown, Vineyard Haven, and Oak Bluffs.

➤ **ATM LOCATIONS: Cirrus** (tel. 800/424–7787). **Plus** (tel. 800/843–7587) for locations in the United States and Canada, or visit your local bank.

➤ **ON MARTHA'S VINEYARD:** ATMs are at the following locations: by the **Compass Bank** (opposite steamship offices in Vineyard Haven and Oak Bluffs; 19 Lower Main St., Edgartown; Up-Island Cronig's Market, State Rd., West Tisbury; tel. 508/693–9400); **Edgartown National Bank** (2 S. Water St. and 251 Upper Main St., tel. 508/627–1140); **Martha's Vineyard Cooperative Bank** (S. Main St., Vineyard Haven, tel. 508/693–0161); and **Park Avenue Mall** (Oak Bluffs, tel. 508/627–1167).

CREDIT CARDS

Throughout this guide, the following abbreviations are used: **AE**, American Express; **D**, Discover; **DC**, Diners Club; **MC**, Master Card; and **V**, Visa.

➤ **REPORTING LOST CARDS:** To report lost or stolen credit cards, call the following toll-free numbers: **American Express** (tel. 800/327–2177); **Discover Card** (tel. 800/347–2683); **Diners Club** (tel. 800/234–6377); **MasterCard** (tel. 800/307–7309); and **Visa** (tel. 800/847–2911).

Packing

Only a few of Martha's Vineyard's restaurants require formal dress. The area prides itself on informality. Do **pack a sweater or jacket, even in summer,** for nights can be cool. For suggested clothing regarding deer ticks and Lyme disease *see* Health, *above*.

In your carry-on luggage **bring an extra pair of eyeglasses or contact lenses** and **enough of any medication you take** to last the entire trip. You may also want your doctor to write a spare prescription using the drug's generic name, since brand names may vary from country to country. In luggage to be checked, **never pack prescription drugs or valuables.** To avoid customs delays, carry medications in their original packaging. And don't forget to copy down and carry addresses of offices that handle refunds of lost traveler's checks.

Perhaps most important of all, **don't forget a swimsuit** (or two).

CHECKING LUGGAGE

How many carry-on bags you can bring with you is up to the airline. Most allow two, but make sure that everything you carry aboard will fit under your seat, and get to the gate early. If you have a seat at the back of the plane, you'll probably board first, while the overhead bins are still empty.

If you are flying internationally, note that baggage allowances may be determined not by piece but by weight—generally 88 pounds (40 kilograms) in first class, 66 pounds (30 kilograms) in business class, and 44 pounds (20 kilograms) in economy.

Airline liability for baggage is limited to $1,250 per person on flights within the United States. On international flights it is $9.07 per pound or $20 per kilogram for checked baggage (roughly $640 per 70-pound bag) and $400 per passenger for unchecked baggage. You can buy additional coverage for about $10 per $1,000 of coverage, but it excludes a rather extensive list of items, shown on your airline ticket.

Before departure **itemize your bags' contents** and their worth, and label the bags with your name, address, and phone number. (If you use your home address, cover it so that potential thieves can't see it readily.) Inside each bag **pack a copy of your itinerary.** At check-in **make sure that each bag is correctly tagged** with the destination airport's three-letter code. If your bags arrive damaged or fail to arrive at all, file a written report with the airline before leaving the airport.

Taxes

SALES TAX
Massachusetts state sales tax is 5%.

Taxis and Limousines

Taxis meet all scheduled ferries and flights, and there are taxi stands by the Flying Horses Carousel in Oak Bluffs, at the foot of Main Street in Edgartown, and by the Steamship office in Vineyard Haven. Fares range from $4 within a town to $35–$40 one-way from Vineyard Haven to Aquinnah. Rates double after midnight. Limousine companies offer service both on- and off-island.

➤ TAXI COMPANIES: **All Island Taxi** (tel. 508/693–2929 or 800/693–8294), **Mario's** (tel. 508/627–6972 or 877/627–6972), **Marlene's** (tel. 508/693–0037 or 800/281–8294), and **Martha's Vineyard Taxi** (tel. 508/693–8660).

➤ BY LIMOUSINE: **Holmes Hole Car Rentals & Limo Service** (36 Water St., Five Corners, Vineyard Haven, tel. 508/693–8838), **Muzik's Limousine Service** (10 Kennebec Ave., Oak Bluffs, tel. 508/693–2212).

Time

Martha's Vineyard is in the Eastern time zone.

Tipping

At restaurants, a 15% tip is standard for waiters; up to 20% may be expected at more expensive establishments. The same goes for taxi drivers, bartenders, and hairdressers. Coat-check operators usually expect $1; bellhops and porters should get 50¢ to $1 per bag; hotel maids in upscale hotels should get about $1.50 per day of your stay. On package tours, conductors and drivers usually get $10 per day from the group as a whole; check whether this has already been figured into your cost. For local sightseeing tours, you may individually tip the driver-guide $1–$5, depending on the length of the tour and the number of people in your party, if he or she has been helpful or informative.

Tour Operators

BUS

The **African-American Heritage Trail** (West Tisbury, tel. 508/693–4361) can be seen on your own, or on tours organized by Elaine Weintraub, a history teacher who created the trail. The trail, which covers the entire island, highlights 14 spots that are important to the history of people of color of Martha's Vineyard. About half the sites are marked with plaques, and include the homes of prominent African American islanders such as the former wife of Adam Clayton Powell, the Shearer Cottage of Oak Bluffs, and outdoor areas where African Americans gathered to worship. The half-day bus tour doesn't leave at specific times, so call for details. If you want to drive and see it yourself, Weintraub's guide to the trail, "African-American Heritage Trail of Martha's Vineyard," is available at bookstores.

Cinnamon Traveler Vineyard Tours (P.O. Box 4803, Oak Bluffs 02568, tel. 718/399–7660 or 508/696–8778) takes visitors on several relaxed island bus tours, including an "All Island Cultural Tour," which highlights spots important to the native Wampanoags and stops on the African-American Heritage Trail. The tours are held during the summer months and led by tour-company managing director and cultural writer Grace Lynis.

CRUISES

The 50-ft sailing catamaran **Arabella** (tel. 508/645–3511) makes day and sunset sails out of Menemsha to Cuttyhunk and the Elizabeth Islands with Captain Hugh Taylor, co-owner of the Outermost Inn.

The teakwood sailing yacht **Ayuthia** (tel. 508/693–7245) offers half-day, full-day, and overnight sails to Nantucket or the Elizabeth Islands out of Coastwise Wharf in Vineyard Haven.

Mad Max (tel. 508/627–7500), a 60-ft high-tech catamaran, offers day sails and charters out of Edgartown.

The **Shenandoah** (tel. 508/693–1699), a square topsail schooner, offers six-day cruises including meals; passengers are ferried to ports, which may include Nantucket, Cuttyhunk, New Bedford, Newport, Block Island, or others. One or two weeks each summer, day sails with lunch are offered (call for schedule). Cruises depart from Coastwise Wharf in Vineyard Haven. "Kids Cruises" (throughout the summer) are for 10- to 18-year-olds only.

FLIGHTSEEING

Warbird Flight (Martha's Vineyard Airport, Edgartown–West Tisbury Rd., West Tisbury, tel. 508/806–9030) will take you on one- or two-hour island tours, including buzzes over Nantucket and Woods Hole on Cape Cod, in a vintage 1948 L-17 warplane.

WALKING

Liz Villard's **Vineyard History Tours** (tel. 508/627–8619) leads walking tours in Oak Bluffs, Vineyard Haven, and Edgartown of "history, architecture, ghosts, and gossip" that include visits to the historic Dr. Daniel Fisher House, the Vincent House, and the Old Whaling Church. Tours are given April–December; call for times. Walks last about an hour.

Visitor Information

Martha's Vineyard Chamber of Commerce (Beach Rd., Box 1698, Vineyard Haven 02568, tel. 508/693–0085, www.mvy.com) is two blocks from the Vineyard Haven ferry. The chamber information booth by the Vineyard Haven steamship terminal is open Memorial Day–last weekend in June, Friday–Sunday 8–8; July–Labor Day, daily 8–8; and Labor Day–Columbus Day, Friday–Sunday 8:30–5:30. The chamber itself is open year-round, weekdays 9–5, with some weekends hours in July and August. There are also town information kiosks on Circuit Avenue in Oak Bluffs and on Church Street in Edgartown.

Web Sites

Do check out the World Wide Web when you're planning. You'll find everything from the latest weather forecast to wedding planners to fishing tips. Fodor's Web site, www.fodors.com, is a great place to start your on-line travels. The various chamber-of-commerce sites are also quite helpful.

➤ WEB SITES: **Martha's Vineyard Chamber of Commerce** (www.mvy.com); **Martha's Vineyard Online** (www.mvol.com); **Massachusetts Office of Travel & Tourism** (www.massvacation.com); **Massachusetts Office of Travel & Tourism** (www.massvacation.com)

Massachusetts Bicycle Coalition (www.massbike.org) for information for bicyclists.

Martha's Vineyard Times (www.mvtimes.com/) has news and listings for community events.

Island ferry information and schedules are available online from the **Steamship Authority** (www.islandferry.com) and from **Hy-Line** (www.hy-linecruises.com).

When to Go

Memorial Day through Labor Day (in some cases Columbus Day) is high season on Martha's Vineyard. This is summer with a capital S, a time for barbecues, beach bumming, water sports, and swimming. During summer everything is open for business on the island, but you can also expect high-season evils: high prices, crowds, and traffic.

The island is, however, increasingly a year-round destination, especially the shoulder seasons of fall and spring, when crowds are few and facilities are open.

CLIMATE
Although there are plenty of idyllic beach days to go around on Martha's Vineyard, rain or fog is not an uncommon part of an August vacation here. Visitors who do not appreciate the beauty of the place in mist and rain may end up mighty cranky.

Temperatures in winter and summer are milder on the Martha's Vineyard than on the mainland. As a rule, the Cape and islands also get much less snow than the mainland. Still, winter can bring bone-chilling dampness.

➤ FORECASTS: For local weather, coastal marine forecasts, and today's tides, call the weather line of **WQRC** in Hyannis (tel. 508/771–5522), or tune in to the Vineyard's **WMVY** (92.7 FM). The **Weather Channel Connection**(tel. 900/932–8437) is 95¢ per minute from a Touch-Tone phone.

CLIMATE

Jan.	40F	+4C	May	62F	17C	Sept.	70F	21C
	25	−4		48	+9		56	13
Feb.	41F	+5C	June	71F	22C	Oct.	59F	15C
	26	−3		56	13		47	8
Mar.	42F	+6C	July	78F	26C	Nov.	49F	9C
	28	−2		63	17		37	3
Apr.	53F	12C	Aug.	76F	24C	Dec.	40F	4C
	40	+4		61	16		26	−3

INDEX

FODOR'S POCKET MARTHA'S VINEYARD

EDITOR: Melissa Klurman

Editorial Contributors: Perry Garfinkel, Karl Luntta, Joyce Wagner

Editorial Production: Marina Padakis/Rebecca Zeiler

Maps: David Lindroth, *cartographer;* Bob Blake and Rebecca Baer, *map editors*

Design: Fabrizio La Rocca, *creative director;* Tigist Getachew, *art director;* Jolie Novak, *senior picture editor*

Production/Manufacturing: Robert B. Shields

Cover Photograph: Richard Pasley/ Stock Boston

COPYRIGHT

First Edition

ISBN 0-679-00783-0

ISSN 1533-0486

IMPORTANT TIP

Although all prices, opening times, and other details in this book are based on information supplied to us at press time, changes occur all the time in the travel world, and Fodor's cannot accept responsibility for facts that become outdated or for inadvertent errors or omissions. So **always confirm information when it matters,** especially if you're making a detour to visit a specific place.

SPECIAL SALES

Fodor's Travel Publications are available at special discounts for bulk purchases for sales promotions or premiums. Special editions, including personalized covers, excerpts of existing guides, and corporate imprints, can be created in large quantities for special needs. For more information, contact your local bookseller or write to Special Markets, Fodor's Travel Publications, 280 Park Avenue, New York, NY 10017. Inquiries from Canada should be directed to your local Canadian bookseller or sent to Random House of Canada, Ltd., Marketing Department, 2775 Matheson Boulevard East, Mississauga, Ontario L4W 4P7. Inquiries from the United Kingdom should be sent to Fodor's Travel Publications, 20 Vauxhall Bridge Road, London SW1V 2SA, England.